SEE YOU THROUGH: A NOVEL

Geoff Gilbert was born in Dunfermline in West Fife and now lives in France, where he works at the American University of Paris. He teaches, writes, and translates, and is currently completing a book on relations between writing and economics, called *For Real*.

Alex Houen was born in Oxford, England, grew up in Sydney, Australia, and teaches in Pembroke College and the Faculty of English, University of Cambridge. He co-edits with Adam Piette the poetry journal *Blackbox Manifold*. His research and writing interests include sacrifice, war literature, affects, and poets' novels.

Also by Geoff Gilbert

Hold West! [with Alex Houen]   (Eyewear, 2016)

Before Modernism Was: Modern History and the Constituency of Writing   (Palgrave Macmillan, 2004)

Also by Alex Houen

Sacrifice and Modern War Writing: Atavisms, Martyrdoms, and Economies of Loss   (OUP, 2024)

Malapartings   (Equipage, 2021)

(Ed.) Affect and Literature   (Cambridge University Press, 2020)

Ring Cycle   (Eyewear, 2018)

Hold West! [with Geoff Gilbert]   *(Eyewear, 2016)*

CONTENTS

HOLD WELL CLEAR   7

CITY LAMENTS   39

TENDER EMAEL VOICE MESSAGES   45

HIM 2 INANA   61

FINDING MIMO   67

PLASTIC ROCK LYRIC   89

SEA'S HEM AND BANLIEUE   95

TENT / CITY   119

SEE YOU THROUGH   127

15 CRITERIA FOR NOVEL GESTURES   157

TAKE GIVE KEEP CARE HOLD WELL CLEAR   161

STOLE SONG   175

ISBN: 978-1-917617-34-5

Cover designed by Aaron Kent

Edited and Typeset by Aaron Kent

Broken Sleep Books Ltd
PO BOX 102
Llandysul
SA44 9BG

See You Through: A Novel

Geoff Gilbert & Alex Houen

Broken Sleep Books

Hold Well Clear

1.   Mimo has work to do, the worst work: checking

live feed that doesn't nourish him

from facial recognition software tied to cameras

around the country. He checks

that the software is working – verifies

tags in Mall CCTV, security in nightclubs,

faces framed for scrutiny. It was from the point

that the voice of his Director began bleeding

into his own inner voice that he found himself

finding the prospect of windows and of memories

irresistible. He needs to get things clear

or get well clear of them – through glass

and plexiglas he sees things differently.

When he moves up to the window and eyes

out, however muffled and uncommon the state he is in,

it is clear where the feelings should be: down there

on the street, sandwiched between other glass panes.

He's watching the arm move

in a shop, stress and compression and stretch,

it rakes what is drifting away (robot blood, fine river sand).

A second arm takes a bottle. With glass you can get away

with a lot of things; but airplane pilots whose eyes

are damaged by plexiglas shards

fare better than those injured by standard glass –

better compatibility between plexiglas and human tissue.

Mimo is intensely interested in how he will look,

in what he will keep.

Your nose is too close to the screen.

There's the Director again, voicing:

A face at a window

for no apparent reason should have a thumb

in its mouth. Or, if the face is not childish it is free-

floating, blotted white by the darkness of the room.

Rub out the formal relations, look through the glass

at the slides we prepared, be ready for chapters

to come in the form of spacing out.

Mimo keeps watching

the arm get confused about the room it is in.

Loss of your own making.

In the majority of applications

plexiglas will not shatter but break

into large dull pieces. Squint through it, glance at it;

what matter? what kind of keep?

what hold? It looked like a sack,

or maybe a deformed animal,

visible behind the middle column, mostly to the right.

It expanded and contracted, pulsing

like some kind of smear.

2.   Loss of your own making. Mimo takes it to heart,

wants so to get it clear to get clear of it, yet

when he tries to take things back he gets an image

of his first aquarium. A shell ricochets in the memory,

sounding his past and catching a stress point

in the screen. Floods of water, plastic forts, weeds and silver-

bellied fish slip and jump around him, pooling

in the room. Those two little round things,

the shape of a bumble-bee, flashing past and displaying

on their rear end a round eye bordered with blue,

are they really fish?

He squeezes his mind firmly,

tries to bring it all back. He can remember

some parental face as it gaped down, remember

the lino, remember how in that moment the structure

of arms corresponds to the structure of legs.

He can put that box back, or he can kneel

to feel surging water. But the fish:

of the dull-coloured kind, or pastel grunts,

he nearly always sees several of the same family at once,

but of the brightly coloured within his field of vision

there is *one* blue and *one* black angel-fish.

Like the hardwood forests, and the songbirds

too, the idea that these fish could cease

while he is 'working', that those might be the last,

brings on an attack of nausea, and he screens
his eyes against them.

I will rip the souped-up spine I added
to your ribs back out of your back before I let you flow away as the loss
of your own making.

When Mimo makes a spectacle of himself
he's learned he needs to pool a little dance and try to keep it
to himself. An aquarium is good measure of a spine's hardness;
ideally they are compatible, descending together towards soft
flesh and its opening: no one ever shattered an ass
to fragments; no one threatens to actually steal your anus.
But it can slip away from you while nobody is watching.
That parental face…

That parental face impresses him
transparency is the best form of detachment:

look me in the face and tell me how you love, loop back
past the one blue and the one black angel-fish to where the crack
began.

He wants a vacation, can't stop looking away.
Designers started building much bigger aquariums when Plexiglas
could be used, but it's been avoided for other large-scale constructions
since the Summerland disaster. Then there's the hardest love
that will never abolish the distance between one window
and another, plus pressure of being already squeezed
between those panes – *Tell me!* – a new slide

every time you try to think – *How you love!*

  To make plexiglas you pour polymerized
methyl methacrylate between two glass panels that are enclosed
by flexible sidebands. During the polymerization process
in a water quench the material shrinks slightly and the glass
plates are drawn towards one another. The finished Plexiglas®
sheet can easily be removed from the glass plates.
'Easy!?', thinks Mimo, needing a break, feeling the screens
and the surfaces form. Nothing novel there.

3.   *Hold well clear.* By that parental gaze

Mimo had realized himself given up – from father

to mother. Distance became form of paternity, with maternity

being this Mesopotamian bottle of dark brown glass

(weathered to grey) and turquoise blue, excavated

from an ancient grave at the Sumerian city of Ur

in Southern Iraq. Mimo squints, tries it

at arm's length then close up to his dark brown eyes.

He's heard of people who can read this stuff,

buried miracles like this as well as the detritus

taken by floods, the trampled shards flung outwards

by migrations, the trace of cleansing fires

and ordinary violence. *Cleansing fires…*

He's never seen a ram hiding in a thicket; to stop himself

thinking of burnt offerings he switches to the aquarium

with its occasional flashes of colourful anger and appeasement.

The rush of hot blood to the Director's face turns his voice

a deep violet:

> *look me in the face! Work!*

                              Mimo's eyes hang still,

resting with the water. But something warms in his face too.

He's tried to leave before but that's going nowhere; every time

they've fallen out they've made up some kind of solution

in which he finds himself suspended, just one of the fish in the tank.

A water conducting gill slit to a sound-conducting hearing tube;

two bones of a jaw joint to two little auditory bones;

a reptile's arm

to a bird's wing.

He's stuck

with this, has given it some thought,

and then been shattered

by the violence of the response,

sheer volume of demand.

Again he ranges evidence before him: broken pieces,

parts of creatures that are dull, and evil lively shards,

and some clear things

in the distance. They have to hold together.

He recalls the dance of cranes: a crane rears up and unfolds

its mighty wings at another, fixing it with eyes and beak;

so far this gesture looks like preparation for attack;

but the next moment the bird turns its back

to the other and presents its vulnerable occiput

which is topped with a little red cap;

it stays in that position for a while to show that its threat

is directed at the terrible world; then it turns again to face

the other crane, performing for it a play attack

on any substitute object – a further crane,

a piece of wood, a stone which it seizes in its beak

and throws three times or four times in the air. He can pass

through glass in this scene, releasing the pathos

in one inferno at least: bodies are crushed

at turnstiles, that had been dancing just minutes before,

polystyrene ceiling tiles melting and dripping their black fire

stupidly on the moment before the whole place went up.

4.   *It has to be said: you've never died, but you've definitely been*
       killed a bit. What do you make of that?

                                              Things go missing
       all the time, however careful he may be. All this surveillance,
       those banks of data, fish filmed through the clear bottom
       of a boat: what's the Director for if not to cut
       this seamlessly together? Mimo has lived for all his life
       with nagging losses of his life, played out
       on screens and dancefloors.

                                      Loss of my own making?
       Sometimes before sleep he sounds out the idea
       of a death that occurs with no body.

                                      It has to be said.
       Writing calls into action a pretty separate character,
       some imaginary friend who speaks silent from the crack
       between what happens and what is?

                                              There is no real
       relationship between us and death; all creatures
       contemplate it with composure, indifference, irresponsibility,
       through the glass bottom of a holiday skiff. So why
       does the imagination of the friend see sad shyness creep
       into Mimo's gentle eyes? Why turn from the boundless
       advantages of disgrace and hide his once so open gaze,
       now dark instinctive shame?

                      You have to get to the bottom of this.

Shame is another way

of being pregnant with imaginary friend,

and that intimacy – so full of love,

desire, drinks, and aggression – may present like a flock

of Christian angels equally responsive to any.

But you were <u>killed</u> a little, more than once.
In Club LammasLand, for instance,
remember how it slipped away, was taken
from you.

The desire and drinks did flow that night,

the field was open to everything, the Blaze and Arca

and samples of Divine. Mimo had flowed out

through it all, surging out and drawing back, close

at hand and trampled under foot.

He thought the moment had been shared,

but he completely lost it.

When he tries to temper himself

to bring it back, he just gets an image of the Club's aquarium,

or that dancing image of Arca on the screen smearing from

her to him to fish and back; he wants an undulant elsewhere,

himself as a cursor, a point in the common sensuality

with his friends. But these are several large dull pieces,

and they half cross his heart with a terrible haste.

If not common sense, then at least some sense held

in severalty? Moments might be the elements of profit,

but at moments like these Mimo pictures himself an ancient

mould-blown glass jar with lattice ribs; someone's arm holding it

up to the light of an open window

then letting it go to greet

the street below. Always the body first,

the dress flamed, the body burnt, a shard

in the eye, the imaginary friend left

at the bar.

       Seeing to the intimacy of poet and imaginary friend

should also solve the enigma of the crime committed

in an enclosed interior you cannot enter

and from which you cannot leave.

5.   So good to have some time out with my little bother Emael.

They're at the stage already where the plastic glass

is slipping from their grip and something goofy

is all over their face. *I love this one* to no one

in particular, and it's my own voice also coming back to me,

shuffling to the heart of the dancefloor. We suck on our blue

fluorescent ice with all we have taken

and watch the dancing bodies blur

in and out of dry-ice smoke. There's a pink laser

cutting through it as cone then plane then lines

and as I watch I feel my spine unlock

so it's not love exactly but a kind of lattice

work for love to climb on. Something is brought to my ears

from deep down in the cavities, the plastic in my knees,

from membranes and from deep down in the language,

one skin round Emael's inner flesh, the music that they move to,

and me.

       I rest my own gaze with the laser on a scapula across the room

and watch it smile then deep down I can feel E say

that's not a heartbeat, this is a heartbeat! and they're mouthing

over and over

        La da dee, la dee da

        La da dee, la dee da

so sweet I can see that we just need

a bit of our own deaths and then to see our friends

sort out their makeup. My present voice is graded with shadow,

richly clothed with bodies that have blocked the light,

and for the moment I can hitch it up and just kick off again,

make it sway around me. I mean, *we* can, as I see that E

has started up again a beat ahead of me.

Their mouthing with me makes me think of those voices

that speak to me without a mouth – my own inner voice

doesn't lie to me but I never know when it's a joke.

      All this dry-ice smoke. Anxiety is a smokescreen

that spares you the need to shed light on stuff

but here goes the laser shedding light again

      and we're off in its wake,

      right across the room,

      left our breath behind.

There's another room here, even more intense, no time

for lungs, the laser finds another wavelength, smooths

all skin and stretches it around some word to come.

      'A story is like music: divides time up,

so there is something to it' – my voice is quoting

those late comments, faded so far that I am unsure

just how long ago it was the speaker moved

among us. Pretty soon E will be leaving me for their

'window of opportunity'

but right now *She's just like you and me/*

As she stands there begging for money and as I'm watching

their mouth this room is all beating skin and spine with us

and skin is dazzling plane of pink smoke

and spine is burning line of pink light,

which may be why I replied to the speaker: 'Fiction

these days has to be a body smoothed with plastic microspheres'.

Bending to an ear

touched with pink, I want to throw in 'plombage' but my lungs

are elsewhere, off with Emael, our colour broadcast strong

because of their amazing tented canopy, ripped off from Munich 72.

When you remember this, don't put it behind glass, just look

at the plexiglas tank, its fish. When you see a grunt

from a distance you see a so-so greenish-silver fish

and only when it's right in front of you

do you notice the gold and sky-blue

hieroglyphs clothing their body like brocade.

I can't tell E how much I want to keep them

close. *I can't tell you how much I want to keep you*

close! and I'm so beside myself with this I switch myself to another

wavelength so I'm unlocking not the love exactly but a

kind of scaffold for it here:

in a purified form, plexiglas is matrix in laser

dye-doped organic solid-state gain media

for tunable solid-state dye lasers;

it aids as a resist in the electron-beam lithography

process; nanostructured plexiglass surface can be easily smoothed by vacuum ultraviolet irradiation;

a blacklight-reactive tattoo ink using plexiglas

microcapsules has been developed; and plexiglas

bone cement doesn't bond

to either the bone

or the implant but fills the spaces

between the prosthesis and the bone

preventing motion!

6.　　Nights like this it all clicks into place. How you see

　　　and how it is are one and moving, E

　　　right at the centre of it all in their mess

　　　of vintages. Something drops away now, stress

　　　and doubt beaten off by the beat; abandoned

　　　populations, dried-up river beds,

　　　the morning at the screen, all gone.

　　　　　　Instead this conviction that Emael is so good

　　　　　　at robbing things of their impersonality: clouds,

　　　　　　skin, ice, clothes, rivers, whatever,

　　　and that animated goldfish-bowl face

　　　they do for themselves on Snap isn't the half of it –

　　　they should have a lava face instead for it's pretty clear

　　　that maternity for Emael is an improvised volcano.

　　　They've stolen that kid there for sure, he's melted,

　　　bright, and flowing down to them.

　　　　　　I love to watch them like this, half my bother half

　　　　　　a crack across my world, everything escapes me

　　　　　　besides them.

　　　I need to keep this to myself, their crime, my love for them,

　　　I need not turn my back on them but must get to the bottom of it.

　　　I need to Romeo their face, project a lot of dots onto it

　　　and then perform a Juliet reading of all its local and global.

7.   *What light!* Still at the window.

Window still. Let day in and life out. Boofh.

What light breaks into. And the memories

not voluntary nor involuntary, but arrested,

contracted? Certainly confined as he is to his shift

for four hours more, memory to be held

all here, not going there. Another coffee

to send the blue ice packing, mind squeezed

to the screen. Oppress the tender thing

to focus on the job in hand. Three

new notifications, all whitelist, go. It's exhausting

doing these landmarks, getting the measure

of their pyramids, their distances –

width of mouth, width of eyes,

pupil to pupil, et cetera, et cetera,

with rotation, lean, tilt and scale

of head all taken into account.

The software keeps the eye, of course, and he just checks

the eye it's keeping, vigilant, so the exhaustion is

the network, not the work, he knows. But the pressure

on his eyeballs so he doesn't account

that woman's lines or her planes,

the way she has a bit of bottle to her,

her fatigue, so he doesn't bend to her ear:

it's straining something in him too.

Your nose is too close to the screen.

                                    Because

he's dimmed it, dimmed it ever since

being on the pier, not being there for ages, gazing

up at sky's blue light and seeing his eye floaters up there

dancing about tracking his gaze wherever he looked

until a wave of panic threw an incredible scale in him

somewhere between agoraphobia

and claustrophobia. He let it rise in him

again that night with Emael, with the pink,

on the ramified brocades, with the flow up

the spines and through the other room, up

the lattice, higher than a satellite

and closer than a conga line of baby shrews

he let it rise.

          Remember how it slipped away.

Two new notifications. Blacklist. Whitelist.

Signal. Go.

          The impersonal character of print

is augmented by its capacity for breaking

into a reader's inner voice. Emael

trying to blow little floating smoke rings

from the pink cones of dry-ice smoke.

Pan, tilt, zoom.

          Now back to notifications:

this one stinks

of error in the Fisherface

process, too much work too early

on the data. It stares him in the face

how wrong it is, he forwards it to Tech,

a mote in their eye, the green brackets lift

from round the boy's face,

he steps out of frame

8.   'While away…' – yes, a very thin partition these days
between bored browsing and witnessing.
This kind of mall feed scan for shoplifters keeps driving
him to his own devices. Buys that book on his phone
then back to a group of laughing girls. *Wayward Lives*,
Prime, yes, immediate; no match yet, the camera keeps
with them. What city even is it? Memphis, Kish,
Esztergorm? The light just takes the edge off
everything except the nodes they measure.

      Ha: 'A big smile can render the whole system less
effective'. Emael grinning as a kid in their bedroom
having graduated from stealing jelly babies to stealing
that pen knife they were obsessed with –
then they were beside themselves making cross sections
of jelly babies, mosaics of jelly babies,
'Sweet solid light'.

              Privilege validated at the Club
on the other screen; yes, straight to VIP for her,
into the members' enclosure with various others
including a king who breaks the frame, possibly a singer,
and bald-headed figures wearing skirts with fringes
who parade their produce, animals and grain and fishes,
and lead equids by ropes attached to nose rings.
Since that live image match last week turned out to be
of someone who died last year he's been feeling

compelled on the street to greet the odd stranger

as the historical person they look like. He's haunted

by the carved wound on the trampled boy,

wants to match him

on the street before it gets too late.

You are flowing away from chapters to come.

Snap back to screens, the movement from parking

to shopping space, the closed set of predicted crimes

and threats, the shift, his living room, the window. Emael

using a lighter to bond the jellied edges together.

'Emael, why can't you just eat them like everyone else?'

'A body is too much of itself'.

Mimo's last identification on the street, two fat balding

middle-aged white guys:

'Alfred … it's really you!'

'Excuse me?'

'Alfrech Hidcock … O man.

I'm such a fan. You're alive, and you've multiplied!'

There's a match on the actual security guard now,

that's no surprise, and phantom face ghosts briefly

on the plexiglas shield between the patron

and the register, then gone.

His eyes drop to his phone again,

stolen time or lost

9.   Back to the site specialising in transparent plexiglas kayaks,

glamping domes, and riot shields 'made of 100% new virgin

polycarbonate sheets'. 'Humanization Design Principle':

'adjustable strap – adjustable according to police arm'.

'Custom riot capture shield shape up to 5 metres' –

to capture Colossal Youth? Enormous waters,

huge skies, resistant energetic masses

held in these curves, brought close enough

to touch the screen they're smeared in.

It's shipping him straight back in time

and under filtered southern light

on fine hot sand, he and Emael

lying in the green light of their green tent,

E lip-synching to their imaginary love, a vein

ticking big in their bicep, exhausted after one of their 'digs'

and parents are nowhere in sight.

He's ordering the fragments, pretending not to watch,

laying edge to edge, shard by shard, and waiting

for the image to appear. It still escapes him,

though the glow from E's warm face comes back,

strong against the green light, and the funk

from the sleeping bag, and the story of the snake

in the lost hat. 'What are you doing?'

E mouth open, undulant, 'I'm kissing',

kissing the air, but looking like a labyrinth fish

about to engage in a mouth fight. Mimo's eyes

drop to the fragments, he flushes, then back to E,

still composing themselves, arranging their jaw

to their rising wings, their spine pure plastic light.

'You crack me up'. They are turning to Mimo now,

about to erupt and immure him, and then they feint

away, back to the business of love.

Out of the air freakish a voice without a face says to Mimo

To live outside of servitude and those who herd

us into fiction...

       Green tent. Green Brackets. Green.

'As we redesign a new world partitioned by plexiglas,

the industry experiences whiplash'. Round riot

shield, French riot shield, Rectangle riot shield,

Anti riot shield. The resemblance he needs to find,

to zone and mark with triangles, with foliage

and with scales, is right there on the other side of these,

annihilating all. Just stay down here with E

beneath the surface of the job,

ignore directions:

       In the name of the people

       I command you to disperse.

What is the job? Weighing up long takes

from no one's POV. When he daydreams

of flocks or herds it's not like flies around a carcass

or winkles settling for a bit of tidal zone;

no, it's the bull-headed Lyres of Ur,

found when the coastline advanced,

when the marshes drained,

with the graveshafts of amulets,

bottles, and pots, and masks

against cameras and the virus and Gutians.

Emael messed up his patterned glass fragments, ate

jelly babies in their place. Out of the air now, no blade

of grass or neighbourhood. The glamping dome bubble

tent has 'marvelous strength to withstand the sudden

stormy', curving as capture shield 'to wrap around

the subject'. The wound of longing

opened deep in Mimo with these songs,

a claustral wish to wrap himself

in heavy light, to turn the screens off,

smell the funk and resin tight on him,

E close on him,

the smoke and mercury preserving him

an incredible scale against the terrible world.

Each lyre has eleven strings to produce a buzzing noise

that repeats throughout this novel.

One new notification:

blacklist. Last look at the site's plexiglas casket:

'a revolutionary way to view the passing of a loved one,

where you can truly see your loved one

for one last time, there is simply nothing

to compare it to'

10.   The directive on this job demands special concentration,

so Mimo puts his phone away, rubs his eyes and groans

back to the screen. He tries to stifle wonderment as faces

charge him with treasures and passions he can't afford.

Ha! The king's guests now taking up animal masks –

fat chance of Fisherface. One is the head of a lion,

another a dragon, another some kind of serpent.

More liberties than he can really take: he stamps the sparks

as soon as they take hold, match serpent

to snake, horse to equid, dragon to low-bellied lizard,

scale back the aura of the king and snap him

to the grid. The gaps in the record are more copious

and richly coloured than the data themselves, green light,

green air, and now, no, you're kidding, not dry-ice

smoke, not with green laser, it's like some kind of plot.

You are not what you see.

You are not when you see.

Perhaps it's because the feed is silent it seems

so spectral or is it these other masks – the mask of flames

the mask of lightning? – throwing a fresh wave

of incredible scale in him. A picture by another hand grafts

on the picture, a lawless incident. It bellies forth,

he's sorting them and daubing them like sheep

and they are devastating him, a breeze

haunts his sheepfold. He's on a woeful wage and his eyes

dare not stray from screen to chance of the street,

or to warmth back in the tent, their faces then.

    Don't drop your gaze.

            It's like the mask of lightning

is doing the lasers, making the venue a face

of itself. What if he *has* dropped his gaze,

dropped it like a ball into a kind of netherworld?

Who will retrieve my gaze?

    Notification.

         Mall feed activity, some young boy

running out of Nike store with a sweatshirt

under his sweatshirt, probe image of him

from the mall detective's phone, yes,

the database match holds up, poor sweetheart,

there he is hiding in Screen 2 by the stairwell

curled up pretending to sleep.

    Please stay with this boy.

         Stay with Emael's

cold panic as it cracked across their mischief

when the fire took, stay close to the carved wound

and the sweat going cold, and pay yourself largely

with words. Nakedness says death here, a shuttle

to the other world, but on the other screen

the king's guests trample on and must be visioned,

each of them bearing their tribute, the hard woods

from the higher land, the hard stones, the metals.

And the pills – look at that, serpent man

definitely just slipped something furtively to an equid.

Just as well the system's algorithmic eye can't see

the big picture, and now judging from the dance moves

the music has reached such a level in the club it's spread

to Screen 2 as the boy is up and running with it.

    Project First. This is not the way the story functions.

Rooting for the boy: he pops the pixels in his mouth,

he brandishes his 2020 tie-dye like a tiny conflagration,

takes to his heels and Mimo sees for a second what he is.

Tie-dye? Looks more like blood stains

and the stains of other fluids.

The boy is a wound waiting to happen.

    Eyes on the prize.

        The third person

the Director wants is a voice so stupid

that it expresses what there is like dust in the wind,

like a breeze in an empty sheepfold.

    Have you watched the king?

    I have.

    How does he fare?

    He inward cries 'O my legs, o my hands!'

    Have you watched the lion?

    I have.

How does he fare?

It's not clear how he got his bones.

Have you watched the thieving boy?

I have.

How does he fare?

You finish a rope, he weeps over the rope.

Did you see him who was set on fire? How does he fare?

I do not see them. Their spirit is not about.

Their smoke went up to the sky.

City Laments

11.   That it should all collapse by itself   like nothing we've seen

before   like something unseen. How long will the foundations

and brickwork strain their eyes upwards in lamentations?

The storm which knows no mother, knows no father,

knows no brother has pushed my righteous house over

on its side like a garden fence and wind   have been made to fall on it

as onto a tent. The swamp has swallowed my possessions

accumulated in the city, the crown on his head and the tiara

have been spoiled   [*lines lost*]   she cried bitterly. City

in another time   they piled up in their crop-tops

and their slashed shorts by the turnstiles, heaped like sheaves,

crushed and darkened to plastic, facets vitrified,

bird's wing held to reptile arm   City is embrace

prised apart. City is not drunk but their heads drooped

anyways on their shoulders. Buildings stand but are no longer

seen as having been built.   Where can I sit?

City lasts.   How long will this last? Days do not pass,

only weeks, but the moment when the music is not played

and the instant when the enemy see the sacred box

that no one had set eyes on is long like a dance remix

in City. All the channels City laments. All the screens frozen

City laments. It is taking a toll on faces. 'I just look tired,

jowly, droopy' cried a Zoom-face sufferer. 'I'm looking older

than I am need filler'. Teme plants grow thick in watercourses

once suitable for barges, and mountain thorn on roads

built for convoys. Somewhere in City the man who used to drill

wells scratches ground at the market place. Mooring-pole

of heaven has been City but City has worn a hole with mooring-pole:

plug-hole of heaven.   People stand but are no longer seen

as having been born and raised.   Where do I stand?

When glass is given a bath of potassium nitrate or sodium nitrate

it is toughened but our skies rain it down

in crunchy drops, forms static river City cannot bathe in,

can't anoint with, can't slake its thirst on, can't slush, see through,

see. This is not my child. This on every channel, freezing

every screen.   That city cannot save life cannot save up

life is stunning to it. Hunger fills City like water where no

water is. City as always is credit is possessions takes credit

for this as possessions like a flock of rooks takes flight.

Where do I stand?   City blows up these days

as 2,750 tons of ammonium nitrate in its port and all the windows

break up and take flight into people. Mountains of glass

are swept from shattered apartments. These are not

compatible, not the shepherd's hut and the winds from the south,

nor the beach and the years to come where you will work

at your screen to hold a palace steady there, against its toppling,

its ceiling to floor windows. Its plans were ordained

and have changed. The hordes in masks and the stranger in the shadow

in a mask they take the dung you stacked and scatter it.

They make your soft flesh tough they shatter your soft flesh,

make you an air of particulate matter. Small glass particles
and rubble embedded in faces and limbs. City is running out
of stitches. Many suffer cuts to eyes and nerves and income and
City does a roar like a jet engine shrouded in broken glass and debris

Tender Emael Voice Messages

12.   Hey fishyface what you up to? Changed your colours yet? Sorry didn't call when I said, I know, been busy with it all. Nightmare. Weird being back. Uncle Jacques's thrown me into the deep end, so much for helping with the website, only potwashing and prep so far, still no money, so thank you for the transfer. Slime and stink all over me and hands are raw.   Night's well weird down here, noises back the cabin creeping me. I wish that you [*inaudible*] again. The guys are ok, don't know what they're jabbering half the time. It honks in there – remember how he packed us in with other kids and 'Dickhead' from Dhi Qar hating you? Argh, called again for shift, late, try you in a bit

𝍖

Hey me again, where you at boy!? Quick break here after an hour on pots and two on squid and octopus, I think it's doing something to my skin, he's got a new one new octopus in the kitchen tank, called it Zinédine, poor thing keeps watching me doing the prep – hey, did you know an octopus can fit through a hole the size of its eye, diving boy Khaled told me. Even the massive ones they spread like carpets skite off like a spaceship they can get themselves into a bottle. It hangs there eyeing me when I'm getting the budgie bit and guts out the squid. Khaled said they're into stuff, they're thinking.   I'm knackered, from just every-thing. Not been out in donkey's years. Old dears slurping urchins in the restaurant. Been out once or twice to help with tables, but Jacques doesn't want me near them, not the grill either.   Been doing some Duolingo like you told me. Can say 'Excuse me, there is a man in your squid'. [*sighs*] Gotta go.

🐙

Hey fuckface, one of yr long shift days? Hope you been snatching some writing time. Just back at the cabin, knackered. You remember Bruno? Still here, still a total phobe, got a new crew of boys he does the dives with back around Calanque. They bring octopus back to the cabins, hang them on the terrace, it's like a fucking curtain of prolapses out there. They bash them in the bath to make them tender! Caught Khaled out with them, touching their arm things tender, head drooped on his shoulders. Says their brains are all over them, they can see and plan and feel remember in every part. Bruno would have pissed himself. Don't know how it works, the money when he sells them on to Jacques and others, but I need my share of the dosh. There's things I want.   Get out at all? Too much time you spend just looking – not good for you! Am maybe going out on the boat tonight, I think they're going to let me. Anyway, look, I'm sorry to ask, I know I know, but could you transfer me just a bit more to keep me going until Jacques pays up? Should be in a day two days, then there's the Bruno thing. It's not for bidding on another ring, I promise

🐙

Hey trampy scampi, ah … you okay? I'm on my way to the restaurant again, split shift. Went out with Bruno and the boys last night. Mostly had me hauling ropes of pots they catch octopus with. Holding the torch. Keeping an eye out, shit like that. Did you manage [*drowned out by breezes*]? Took a while to get there, engines off to keep quiet, inky black dark out there, and sound of cicadas. Took me back. Khaled [*drowned out by breezes*]. So they made me do this thing, said it was best to just bite it between the eyes where the brain is or something, they kind of mimed it in torchlight, have to do it quick or they're off through the cracks, and Bruno laughing saying 'suck it in to back of mouth and bite'. There's me holding the first fucker we pull out, it's twining up my arm gripping my ear and after I get hold of it right I'm like *chomp* right through its fucking head. Wait. [*long pause*] Just got a message: I got the ring! Fuck. Mimo sweet you need to send me some money pronto, okay? So they're all cracking up trying to keep quiet and I can feel Khaled melting weird, flowing to my face covering me the suckers and slime. Tasted ok [*the octopus is suffused with nervousness*]. Winked at him and smiled. Then all the other ones they pulled out they just gave it a knife slash to the neck – bosh! done! Fuckers. Look, sorry about the money. Pay you back when Bruno's sold the batch after they've dried. *Une maison est une poulpe*, as we like to say over here.

Big love

13   You should see my tan now Mimo, with new gold against it. Skin's cleared up with all the fish and veg I been eating, looking good! Those scenes you told me you were writing haunting me here, I can see the faces twisted and the buried glass. I started telling Zinédine the story of the trampled boy, the lock cut off the gate. I'm growing a soft spot for him, and when I go near the tank he seems to wave an arm at me, not sure if it's his sex arm – they have a sex arm! Khaled told me. Am seeing them different after what you said about their skin being both all eye and all screen. He doesn't want to be there either but like he's sparing me the pain, till we crack this and then off, like birds in fright! Was good to hear from Nin-girl too – I told you right she called? Still soothing the emo kids and the goth kids, still raging. Went quiet though when I said what they do to octopus to make them tender, how we slam them on the bathtub. Go see Nin. She trusts you. Got to go Mimo, that's Auntie Ish outside in the car. *A plus!*

🐙

Hey big brother, I don't really have anything to say so I thought I'd call and say it, I know how much you love that. Long shift on pots then doing squid again I think it's the ink I find hardest. Jacques shouted at me when I went over to the grill to help out grill boy Omar when the heat was on. Surrounded by men all the time! Nin sent me a bunch of images of her cactus no text. I think she might be hitting the booze hard again, let me know when you've seen her right? She's so great when she's on one, but all the things she has to see and everything she has to touch it starts to bottle up a bit. You should quit that job of yours too – get me, sage of the South – you start to look at all those faces like you can't save one of them. Khaled showed me how long he's underwater when he dives. He does a kind of trance thing first, there's no life through his skin at all, his hands and feet go cold, and then he's gone for seems like ever. First time, even me, you know I coast like fuck, but I tiny panicked when the water just stayed smooth on him. But now I hold my breath up on the boat to stay close to him down there and he reckons if I practise with him a month I'll be able to hold for five minutes. Just need to run a mantra through my mind when doing it, and what came to mind was *Take Give Keep Care Hold Well Clear*. That's right, breath becoming a *thing* for me. Fucking Bruno's noticed how I'm soft on Khaled, was teasing me at dinner in the cabin jabbing at my lazuli with his porky fingers, called me 'soft girl', the other night. '"They?" – non, "they" no good for you, better "it", now … eat!' Idiot.

🕺

This is going to make you squirm so buckle up, Butcho Mucho. I had the best night last night. So we're both just done in with the constant Bruno banter and the long shifts and something tense that's in the air these days. Too hot to sleep, I see Khal awake and looking at the ceiling and just ready. So we head down to the cove and it's cooler by the water and his crazy tattoo wound on tight skin over heart. I get him to slow it beating, then he pulls my hands to his throat, there's no panic in his body, but a kind of fire I can feel in him with his cold arms everywhere around me, and I pull his hands to my throat and start the mantra to hold and suddenly our kissing it's like we're holding each other's breath, I know, sounds cheesy, but then my head's burning with him and his face is flaming up in me then other faces yours Nin's mine Zinédine's faces you've unseen. Woah lost it there a bit. Went way deep under. Take care Mimo keep well!

14.   Hey main manatee, I can't believe you recognized David
        Attenborough in Aldi, hope you gave him my love. So
        they've just announced new lockdown measures here, all
        bars and restaurants to close by the weekend. Jacques, Ish,
        Bruno – all absolutely fuming. When they were shouting in
        my face about it, like it was somehow my fault, like times
        I've been fired and didn't understand, you know what? I
        found myself holding my breath again. First I thought it
        was like just not wanting to get virus – the other day Omar
        freaked at not having his mask when Zinédine spurted at
        him. It wasn't that, it's like I was back being a kid, do you
        remember how I used to hold my breath when grown-ups
        talked to me? I'd totally forgotten about it. They're yab-
        bering away at me quickfire and I'm just holding on. So it
        happened later as well when I went down the cellar to ask
        Ish why they won't let me borrow the car, and she's saying
        something about insurance and not used to the roads and
        there I am again holding my breath and with the holding
        I was making myself a photo of her kind of, holding her,
        holding her at distance, kind of frozen, but her face looked
        like mosaic, jewels, lion-face from way back, streaked with
        tears, and some voice like Ish's saying *here you go: the fold of a
        stole, the opening of a fan, the sparkle of a chandelier.* I was miles
        away with her. It's getting trippy here, Mimo. You should
        write this down in your books. Get back at me when you
        can. Miss you Fishface!

                            🧍

Hey yo! Mimo! Sorry we keep missing each other. You didn't say if you'd got through to Nin. Let me know. Yes, am still seeing Khaled, yes it's fine, and no, still isn't serious, you know me. Things still heating up here about the confinement that's coming. Jacques and Bruno planning to join the anti-Paris protest and Jacques worried about the business going under. So yesterday he wrote numbers on a bunch of pingpong balls and chucked them into Zinédine's tank thinking the ones Zinny touched first would be lottery winners. Fucking desperate old bastard.   I've been feeling a bit for Zinny he seems to be hiding a lot. Ish said he's just old and needs to keep working like the rest of us. It's slacker in the restaurant already, so I'm spending more time at his tank, slowing down my heart and kind of going under with him, practising the mantra, arms tasting the air. I swear we glow a little bit together, and this time voice is right between us. This morning I got: *hold clear, integument in amber, flushes of traffic, frame clipped.* What?! Somehow have to get through this. The brightness here is crazy, really glad I came and all, and anyway we know I couldn't stay. But it's a lot to take in. Speaking of taking, I think Bruno's fucking stolen my ring, the garnet one I just got. So last night we were out on the boats for last haul before closure, Bruno being real snippy, kept calling me 'soft boy'. Very windy choppy out there, and when I held Khaled's breath to get to the bottom the photograph I made myself was rockscape, powdered fragrant lavender, a deep inclusion safe from view. The voice I got went *fancy cut, princess cut, Asscher cut, step cut* like I was still learning the jewellery, it freaked me a bit and I drank too much back at the cabin. So maybe I'd already lost the ring and didn't realise but I reckon Bruno's got it seeing as he asked where it was. Still no news from Nin?

ⵌ

Hey brother. I was listening to that message I sent you earlier and I know I sound kinda crazy, so I don't want you to worry but I didn't say the half of it. When we got back Bruno had me bash the octopus in the bath, he knows I don't like it, and I'd been practising my holding underwater right there in the bath the night before. Khaled came in to help me but Bruno insisted it was mine to do, made me furious, so I kept on drinking, and I thought maybe if I hold breath I'll keep calm, I was so pissed but I got the voice clear again going *heart cut old mine cut rose cut* and then just *princess cut* over and over and when I'd finished with the octopus there I was with just the picture I made me of it all: orange lozenge burns into lime cabochon, stinging blue rough strips, the frame burst by his head and all the tributary baggage piled up. And tears, there were tears coming down my face, but it's like the weeping wasn't mine, was streaming out of the picture. I don't know. Mimo, I don't know! What do you make of it? Don't know how to get out from all the arms, their tender arms here. Now Zinédine is distant and I think I might have to look for other work if things keep going on like this. I can do the work, but

15. Re: soft bother

Hey Mimo,

I got yr messages, sorry for the radio silence. Work's been really tough lately, I've been trying to sort a bunch of really tricky cases that went off the rails with lockdown. Poor kids. Anyway, I finally did some Facetime with Emael yesterday, and they were nattering away as usual, both of us really pleased to see each other, and they told me loads of stuff – the work, that hot thing Khaled they're smitten with, even if they laugh it off, and the nighttimes on the boat.

They were really fidgety though Mimo, kept looking past the screen, and twice their eyes welled up, a massive tear just rolling down their cheek while they were telling tales of sunshine paradise. They need some watching, fuck knows we all do these days. Said something about this march they went on, but they garbled it, went quiet for a bit, then back to joking and showing me those crazy rings. Maybe it's nothing, but the only ever time I've seen them cry in all the years we've known each other is at that Ariana Grande concert, and that was from joy, you know what I mean? Something not right.

I hope all's well with you. Let's meet up soon.

Saturday could work?

Nin xox

Hey my calamimo, good, I'm glad Nin's been in touch. Sure, let's catch up tonight, I'm planning on a quiet one back in the cabin. Just to warn you: I've a bit of a black eye from the stupid protest yesterday. Khaled and I tagged along. Crowds of people down the Canebière, Jacques carrying a sign 'We want to Work!', people banging pots and pans, others calling for another revolution. All those pasty white faces facing one way breathing spitting filling air with bitter so it stings your eyes and you can taste it in your mouth. So I'm clinging on to Khaled *take keep hold* and rubbing at my rings and it's all so hard around me, over me. All these fuckers turning the whole event into an anti-mask thing, and riot police are swarming round with shields and trying to break us up, clear space for a bunch of barefaced RN fuckers, screaming '*Liberté! Liberté!*' it was just horrible, and Bruno's in his element, of course, his dark shirt drinking sweat, he's found his friends and they keep chanting '*Liberté! Liberté!*', but then I saw Maria, you know, from the Tapas place, and she was dancing flamenco to friends, so I took Khaled over to watch for some calm out of the way, he's holding my hand and I'm holding my breath, and she's being still with the music letting her dress do the dancing, folding and refolding, now she's a fountain, now she's a flame, now she's a butterfly – breathtaking! – so we are in our bubble for a glorious moment, felt like clubbing, felt like verdant isles beyond the earth's green, then a police shield on my back shoves me forward, losing Khaled's hand, now face to face with stinking Bruno. I flare up, *the air is full of roughness, my name is fading* and he punches me right in the fucking face and sweeps off with his crowd. An idle word that makes no sense is planted in my heart and kindling there, and I was still, Maria more still now than ever, Khaled stock still. Oh woah Mimo. What a fucking day. Well speak soon.

𓁿

Hey my big goujon, I'm sorry I clammed up at the end, it's just … all a bit much, okay. And Bruno came in larding around so I didn't want to talk about it any more. [*long pause*] Khaled said something the other day: you can't lie to water. I told you Zinédine's been hiding in his tank, right? So this morning I was telling him about Bruno, no one else in the kitchen, and when he came to the glass his eyes were just too much, I found myself holding my breath again, can't help myself, and there I am, making myself a photo, Zinédine dancing still with a voice between us *the foam that's fringed, the hair that's displayed, the smoke that clears.* Fuck me what is this voice?   My own hair's looking great now, getting blonder, so the earrings look amazing. Had this dream last night, way down under in the cove with Khaled, and the pressure on my ears sometimes was ringing like the dinner bell and sometimes Ariana, then Khaled's gone, he's covered his body with rocks and shells and jewels, and I'm trying to get through to him. You bite the lips, you clash your mouth on mouth, then a shark just nosing on him, and then I'm battering his arms his head against a porcelain surface, because his bones are obstacles, I'm trying to tear off part of him for me, I think I've entered in and passed away but the picture of a face rises up and bangs me in the eye, and it isn't Khaled isn't me, the crowd takes him away, his suckers on my face, and I taste terrible to him, my jewels taste terrible, something bitter spreading through the water. When I surfaced awake I went over to Khaled's bed, no one else up, and I was so thirsty for his images to surface to his skin and come away with my stroking him soft so as not to wake him but they wouldn't, just my thirst kept burning away in my frame. So I went and checked out a new ring I'm keeping an eye on, how do they describe it? 'In the centre of the crown we find the face of the jellyfish goddess' – there's a jellyfish goddess! – I want to win it for Khaled. O Mimo, I've said it before: a body is just too much of itself. And that's why it cannot lie to water, and that's why the smoke always clears

Him 2 Inana

16.   In an adjective, in an adverb, in a noun.

      When he wanted to deck his city with gold, with fine lines

      of tiny turquoises and pearls to mark the borough limits

      or to give directions, there was no trade yet

      to bring them to him, so he called to you.

      When the mountain was too mighty and too beautiful,

      when it held its nose far above the ground and would not press lips

      to the dust, you strapped on your sandals

      and with your speed and chaos you cleared the horizon

      of everything inanimate that was as glorious as you,

      and in an instant any two eyes were remote

      from each other, left grasping at distance as you

      sipped inappeasible as bees at all the sweets.

      The frame of this world shuddered strings of tubular beads,

      garlands of gold leaves, crest of stylized

      gold flowers with every shake of your head-dress.

      Steal everything from me! Leave me drunk and without

      any wisdom, slap down my monsters, so I can resonate

      over empty spaces, on scorched earth, can slight fat

      pastures to moo on hollow through the ashes

      in the place you made for me to feel in. I bake

      fat-hipped cakes to your form in the burning ground.

      Even your absence from me, even your leaving me

      with nothing makes me fond and personal.

      When the useless gardener violated you under the only tree

he hadn't killed, we all thrilled to the universe you built

and mapped to waste him in. When you made your shining,

when you princess-cut your losses, when you made your genitals

remarkable you deserved to skipper the Boat of Heaven.

In an instant, craft of scribe of smith of builder of information

technology were yours. You received kindling, embers,

extinguishers, care, counselling, sheepfold, breezes, deceit,

strife, kindness, kisses, running – all to give. I camouflagellate

to cover myself in your path. In admiration, your hairstyle,

in admiration, my feet not wet my hands not wet,

your hairstyle. The wound on the page was the wound

on the calf, over his heart through taut skin

flashed through from your terrible radiance, your forthright speech,

deceitful speech, botposts, your plundering of cities, running.

These holes you breach in us are punctures in angles

from heart to navel, from ear to eye, brow to nostril, mooring pole

to plughole. Where is the Boat of Heaven now?

Give me please more holes, make me all hole:

for the fear you forced the mountain range to feel,

for your strength with measuring rod and pepper spray,

for the shaking of your head-dress and the jewellery

you had Vesuvius preserve I have made cluster earrings

of small pearls and emerald beads

threaded into a ball suspended

from my pierced skin on gold vertical wire. I yearn

to copy you, craft suspension of infidelity as our other form

of belief, in an adjective, in an adverb, in a noun.

I just manage swallow where you were swan, I'm a child

racing cheetah, I'm laughably like you, a vessel leaking you

through me, cannot ever be filled. I try to go as one

who brings forth chocolate and the very guts

of battle. When I am at a quarreling place

I am a figurine brought to life. When I sit in the pub

I am an exuberant woman and a young man.

Even when I drink from puddles with the dogs

your dwelling flames up in my frame. A person

is at least two remote things grasped in their maximum

distance. I crave your voice in writing

Finding Mimo

17.   Buzz buzz, yes, hello hello, here we go, I'm ready.

    I think that perhaps you are not there or anywhere
to be written.

        Fuck that, I know where I stand, can see
that glass is a question not so much of quantity as quality;
a question not of how many but of order. Mimo
at his window, at his screen, shifting uneasy on his chair
as he starts up, logs on, prepares for it all to stream on through.
His performance targets on the dashboard, the grid of images
he barely has to look at, faces framed and checked and stored,
a face enters bottom left, moves away from another angle
centre-right, back in again at the top of the screen, head on.

        So what are they saying about this new algorithm designed
'with masks in mind'? 'This solution can manage the entire life-
cycle of identification from enrollment of population to issuance
of a unique ID'. No matching this evening, just reporting
on how it's working. Yes – same person, Yes – left of face
and right of face same face, Yes – same. No – bollard with a hat,
No – shadow on a riot shield, No – drawing of Johnson on a placard.
No – . No, a child. When Mimo thinks the life-cycle of a positive ID
what comes to mind is Emael sending him a link to caddisfly larvae
making themselves cocoons with bits of gold, pearl, and turquoise.
He's been inside these images, training trips to London,
shit drinks with colleagues in that All Bar One, free afternoon
at the portraits – Hayek looking stoned by Moynihan,

against a grand rush of nicotine gold wall, sliding right.

Doesn't usually find his places in the feed, and he mustn't run

his memories in here beside that girl ('No justice, No peace'),

Yes – face, Yes – same.

Training the eager software,

sinking like a diver, 'ensured by a combination of convolutional

neural networks that utilise most up to date architecture'.

So is it economics, this protest? Maybe people pooling

in the name of hardest love. Hard to make out

from the other placards: 'Freedom!' 'Furloughs for Longer!'

'I Can't Breathe'.

Careful, this scene of complication should be kept

distanced and indistinct for plot to move through.

La longue haleine.

She's squeezed now, almost off her feet,

moved sideways by the mass moving off from Trafalgar Square,

all sandwiched and surprised by riot shields and the territory.

The part of face he sees keeps something back which could be joy.

[*she is purged in big being*]. Not to my eyes, she's dancing #metoo

with Extinction Rebellion from last year, with Tanguy

and Jad in Dijon in 2005, with 2011 anti-cuts protests,

with St Louis 2017 and everywhere now at this time. Man

clambering down from Nelson's Column with his 'Rise Like Lions

After Slumber' placard. Boy in a hoodie cycling towards the police

by Edith Cavell statue doing a wheelie. No, the weapons detection clearly isn't working: banana, plastic waterbottle, waterbottle,

folded mini umbrella, umbrella, umbrella, bottle …

what a mess, and too many probe images flashing up

to be on some safe side. Where is he in this mess,

as they kettle her between gallery and probe? Only subjects

of recognition can be proper objects of recognition. No –

child. A surge wheels down the Strand, a flurry of faults, Emael –

their mouth moving across the room – matches dug up

without rhyme or reason. She's with her friends, their chant

is not part of the feed, they flow into another current, more

friends, pain, fear, joy, and for some reason a sense that these

might soon be 'aerosolized'. Ha, good placard 'No Chance!'

near the Museum of Happiness, Wheelie Boy off now

towards the Strand, and look what's down there: Coutts Bank, Topshop,

The Whisky Exchange, National Grid, and the police

are surely going to go over the top because this all comes down

to glass, the glass that orders the world and so is political

but impossible to establish because it's a risk masquerading

as promise. Mimo lays his clammy hands over his eyes and savours

a green moment of these images smashed into bright pieces

and then joined again inside his head. If he had more hands

he would stop his ears against the clamouring alerts,

the eager software begging to be trained,

the ringing gone inside. Terrained.

A homeless woman moving unwatched to the edge

with her dog drinking from the gutter

18.   He's the agent of flat recognition

of these people

of a particular kind

forever, selling their attention too.

This edge is hard, the high degree of improvisation

and suddenness comes through as a feeling

of elation and freedom, all so quick it's hard to know

where anyone would slip in an advertising spot,

or a fresh prompt. The police present their screens,

plexiglas spikes itself flat on the incarnated

density of these moments. Her face once again and

She's just like you and me

As she stands there...?

Well, not sure he can tell real-time

right now with her there clinging

to a traffic-light orange burning

to ruby cabochon, Yes — little roses

on the little rose bush, remote control,

bunch of pine cones, motes of DNA fluff, halogen

bulb, silica, a voice without a face – yes these here too

are my body its senses its feelings tearing-off

and tearing-up, these hopes I do not understand. Diesel

is cheaper than petrol but she can't set fire to a moped

with a can of diesel, it pools dark on the ground

and the flaming rags they sputter and then fade.

This novel is going nowhere. Try to make a scene.

Just do your job!

I want to make a model of the riot

out of couscous. I want to pan slowly up the riot

from sewer to Jupiter's satellite moons. I want to wear the riot

on my buttonhole, sew bits of the riot

into my underclothes. The arc of her foot swinging

set in a block of plexiglas with all the swarming torn-off senses

too as insects, coins, and vials of toxic chemical.

Always body first to body out. And I want to hold

like breath that block as interior you can't enter

and from which you can't leave

bearing little placards like 'Wage, Wage

Against the Dying of the Light', and

'Eat Nowt to Help Out'. I don't want

just to be endlessly pushing the button that used to make

small parts of the scene light up like stained glass at midday

in the model of the whole riot, seven hundred years of riot,

in the plexiglas cabinet at the Museum of London.

We must take our distance to notice what is lost.

No — child.

This procession bears tributary sacks of no grain,

the zigzag wounds on one breast flash

onwards through the composition.

If it does not enter it it is not in it it is out of it and so it enters it.

I need them mouthing with me, setting block on block

and fusing their edges, the room and the street and the screen;

screen street room. And they are! Here's one

downing backpack of rocks by Coutts, police

struggling to kettle a swarm by Itsu

                              Woah! flailing

with edges of shields, three, four people on the ground and

now some rage gathering around them

and there go the windows of Jigsaw

with garments pulled as torn-off people

more police charging over bearing round riot

shields as contact lenses through which to see clothes

or rifle or whisky or fridge or umbrella

as if any want is adjustable according to police arm.

His ergonomic mouse is strange in his hand.

His pine cones. Composition is not there,

it is going to be there and we are here, our own clothes

ripping imperceptible, our window glass not

shattered yet, our rocks with veins of turquoise

and of lapis unmined, our screens our screens our screens

too much of itself.

> *Enough! Did you see the one caught stealing cashmere?*
> I did.
> *How does he fare?*
> Polyester.

Did you see the one winded by shield's edge?

Yes.

How does she fare?

Peeled like garlic.

Did you see the one who felt their ribs to be crowbars for letting light through?

Yes I did.

How do they fare?

They lie stretched on an Ikea futon of the gods.

Did you see the one who threw the fireworks?

Yes.

How does she fare?

Carnation. Green carnation.

19.   *There are those that never appear in mirrors, but only in police*

        cameras. Another writer said that while he was alive

        in Mimo's notebook, at times a hut for him, sometimes

        a kind of broken tent. There is a bit of him to hold to, a smear

        on window, smear on screen, smear on plexiglas shield, floating

        in his vision making ripples of a rising panic

        on which several kinds of waste bob wasteful.

        But all the pressure is to look on through to where his meagre wage

        comes from: my pooled dances? *No.* From seas, from windsweep?

        No. From the Flint Glassmaker's Strikes? *No.*

        From the reflective layer of cells called the *tapetum lucidum*

        ('bright tapestry') next to the retina in shark's eyes? *No.*

        From some kind of surplus, precarious by no windows,

        the hut of temporary construction and the impossible visions

        it gives access to? *No. Still No.* From the hair still wet in curlers

        so she could not go – her mythical sister also could not go –

        and by that chance was uncarbonized the morning after

        unlike those so many other, two bright spots only, eyes

        and buckle?

                No. Wages stretch from the Director,

        they are orientation. Wage surveys. It turnstiles.

                                        And so body

        must be made daily just in time because body is

        more than alive – just think of the flagellate *Euglena* swimming forward

        rotating on its body axis, its orientation done by two organelles, a light-sensitive area in the protoplasm and a bright red stigma

(eye spot), and how, with rotation, the stigma casts a shadow

on the sensitive area causing a beat of the flagellum, until

the creature finally swims straight towards the light.

Mimo's smearing all over his work, smudged

on her cheekbones as she lobs another something

out of frame, he's blurred bright on the spokes of Bicycle Boy

who starfishes across four windows in four directions,

he's fishmouth-marking O on the screen where bubbles rise

as slogan (is that scared or is it sacred? 9 to 5 or 5 to 7?).

Keep it in the tank. I'll dock you. I will garnish.

Something shatters

and something surges and he's back in line. Yes,

when world means no principle and no end in sight there the police

amass holding on to plexiglas as ordered transparency that is in place

as taking place and so, yes, clearly the windows must go.

There is a difference between holding something because you don't

have it, and grasping something because you want it,

and now with the windows of Vodafone and Gee Ricci Menswear

and House of Gifts all down and out here come the police mounted

on equids ready to charge that thin black wall of umbrellas

and cardboard placards by Apples Strand as Backpack Man reaches

for another rock and is that a molotov cocktail being lit by serpent,

legs astride the wounded boy?

There are too many faces now

to match in real time, each backed by one vulnerable occiput.

They'll work this through he knows after the event, the whole thing

kicked upstairs. Police take their screens forwards, police

attempt to move the party to another level.

An invitation to dance is issued from a megaphone.

The sad gas lobs and phuts and whistles in and movement

is friezed. Visibility is police now, screens catch parts

of clutching only, a smile on a scapula, and movements

ordinate towards the other room, too many

for the frame. They're piling at an exit

not an exit, I think the music might have burned out,

but the lighting is amazing, teargas clouds tending to pool

of petrol fire dangling all scribbled over

with green laser pens by two balaclava

boys in search of police eyes or equid eyes the boys

bearing their marvelous strength for withstanding the stormy

as a glamping dome and is that a ram hiding in a thicket?

The weapons detection is beside itself with umbrellas.

Mimo again, surging out and drawing back,

can kneel to feel surging water

or can pause screen 5 for another block

of plexiglas frieze before the police are all beating skin

and spine. And there she is again, stock still

staring at her reflection where the Jigsaw window is gone

or maybe here realizing she can truly see

her loved one.

    Screen flashes obligatory twenty-minute break,

hunger wakes, he logs-off as he must, steps over excavated

fragments on the carpet by the mugs.

He stairs down four flights to the door and out

into this other street. Turns left and slams hard into no riot

at all, air full of no tear gas, light weak through English cloud.

A wave of scale is thrown from him on the silent street,

past Prêt, past masked and distanced, into corner shop

to choose and heat and pay contactless,

weak smile through his mask,

for Emael's favourite Ginster's pasty

20.   So here he goes again, making believe he's working,

looks like it's going to be hard with this shift, why so little

info for the job: three screens on a church entrance,

just monitor the blacklist matching, then event's to cut

to three screens from cameras set up in a cemetery.

Raining now, and it looks like the rain has scratched and scratched away

at massive stone to leave this church.

                                     'St Mary the Virgin'?

There's something noisy from before at the edges of his eyes,

the city fog, the silence hanging on, some urgent crumbs

of pasty, but his simply to follow vaguely these stooped men

blinking as they come out of the church.

They say you may say 'athirst', may say 'not made with hands',

or 'patiently', or 'summer holiday', then later together 'sinner'

is good and 'mercy', and 'out of my depths' or 'I bought a silk

to please you', but he has to guess what they are saying now.

The tall one – hang on, is that Barry Gibb!? – Gibb removing

mask and distancing from Una Stubbs against stone

and flint walls, half an eye for paparazzi, pronouncing 'Joy

has left its stonework, how long will the stonework strain its eyes?'

And she briefly removing mask to reply 'Its paradigm is probably

a woman's breast'. All others masked. No, wait, this other wanting

cool air – can that be Sting? Sting saying to an unmasked nodding

Morrissey, 'if we could find a cure for glass what would we not be

capable of…'. And Morrissey opens his black umbrella, replies

'This is a temple that knows voices. I felt in there the old simplicity:
fire is found in the eyes, air in the tongue, earth in the hands,
and water in the genitals…'

                    Is Mimo actually being moved
by these leathery remnants easy in their frames,
milling by the narthex, shameless as screens?
Una of the Garden City, low rent high wage, low price no sweat,
or lying idle, no public spirit, hands idle, fogs and drought,
costly drainage through torrential rain five cars and still unshattered.
Barry of the grant from Spinning Mule spent bleaching.
This gathered, this celebrity, this passed.

                            Rain is spacing out
all over the umbrellas the social distancing bringing sky down
to earth to make sky, like style, at least two persons.
All masks on and then, no, is that Olivia Newton-John
removing hers in tears to say, 'I, not destroyed by storms,
my attractiveness still going … while I was in charge of …
during the day, the shadows…'. Unable to go on,
so another reveals herself to be Sue Barker saying
'It's as if we're in the place where our mothers laboured'.

        Mimo doesn't know if he can continue, hears *Don't
drop your gaze again!* Desperately wants some ocular shift, maybe
as a baby flounder starting with one eye on each side of its face,
then one eye migrating to the other side of the face
to become mature, the entire migration taking just five days

if you're a starry flounder, and less than one day for other species.

You have the scars but you have no knowledge.

If you're Barry or Harry then cliff in no time because cliff face

because rock. You go downstairs to be introduced

to the future and there's a coffin, and the wall turns,

and there are Stones just everywhere, and lithic paparazzi.

This thing you want to weep for keeps showing up in the rock record,

time stored in the form of fossils like these. Stark choice:

press rock to make glass to make flint to scrape another church.

Or plastiglomerate, setting what we don't get right in plastic stones.

Barry has split from the flock removed his mask and broken

into song, looks like

'Would you believe me if I told you

your tomorrow is my yesterday'

and now emerging from narthex are six in black all masked

slowly bearing what looks like a plexiglas casket

all three screens on it, and Barry singing

'Living eyes, when out in the rain will fall

The day I deny the face of my love'

and oh my its inhabitant in white suit and the face in couscous gold,

yes, it is Cliff Richard, and Mimo now can see

that underneath her mask Sue Barker is saying to herself

'Perhaps until now there really haven't been any bodies'

21.   It's a lot for the ground to take, Cliff in a plastic box,

winched down hole dug

through matter that hasn't settled,

that is still opening with worms

to many futures, that is unsurprised

to be turned up

and distanced from the layers below.

Is not there one thing only that binds gold to gold?

Stones are stuck together by mortar

so stone can learn to crack. Wood held so well

by bull's glue that the veins themselves of the wood

will gape before the binding of the glue will loosen.

How can the Director be so adamant

that you are not what or when you see? Adamant

– and Mimo's mind turns at the word to metal,

its crystals shaped not as gems',

its intercrystalline spaces

the vacancy of metal and its life

with complex plays of spreading cracks, these cracks

a function of certain defects within its crystals.

Defects of line.

Another gaping hole opened to the netherworld

walled with plexiglas, and Cliff sent down

to look around and report back.

Cherie Blair turns to Tony, shakes her head

against this gravity,

      'it's not *my* business to choose the friends

      of my friends'.

But the line has passed at just that moment

through her ring finger, joining it to high branches

of the one remaining uncorrupted yew. The air is full

of painful visibility, rising noxious from the hole,

dispelling all the air in conical pattern

from the grave to a patch of heaven

in which for now no bird could sustain flight.

Torn-off senses tearing. The six in black

holding the casket aloft by its flagella

to ensure it doesn't overly rotate on the body axis.

Cliff in a capsule readied and steadied to be Gaianaut.

It's hard to believe that he has truly transitioned

from the world of glass and its memorabilia:

      'Cliff Richard 75th Birthday Tour Boxed

      Champagne Glasses. Starting Bid £25.

      Unused and in Superb Condition'; 'Cliff Richard

      Glass Xmas Tree Baubles £29.50: Silky Matt Glass

      with Period Images of CLIFF on a Clear Glass Area

      Showing the Silvered Interior

      and Sprinkled with Gold Glitter in a Box

      Covered in 1960s Wrapping Paper.

      The Whole is in Lovely Condition'.

What poison gold mines may exhale, how strange

they make men's faces, how they change

their colour. This smell – its visibility – to Mimo

is a slaughtering blow, the riot in couscous,

Cliff's rictus in glittering couscous,

grain futures and Berber settlements,

horrendous accumulations of this blighted epoch.

To many things sudden calamity and filthy poverty

prompt men: the ulcerations on their skin are loud

across the vision of the cameras,

within the capture of his screen.

Eight decades of unexceptionable hits!

Olivia Newton-John looks shut off from life

by the exceeding delights of the water.

Although her skin is unbroken and is lukewarm

to the touch, her inward parts are burning

to the bones, lines holding her to volcano

and to magma, cracks jointing her

to plastic rocks. She's barely holding herself together

now and Sue Barker is barely holding herself together

and the six in black are barely holding on to Cliff,

lowering him down.

     Yes, there really is a difference

between holding something because you don't have it,

and grasping something because you want it. Barry

is doing what looks like Cliff's 'Milennium Prayer'

making Sting think 'Who has that much breath?'

as Morrissey mutters 'Like a fish in a cistern' while Blair

is mulling over bodies crossing the threshold

back to the world of stone in form of fossil:

> 'And did thou once frequent the sea … did at that fracture
>
> once joint a tail? Did gills the needful air provide, or nostrils
>
> pray?'

> Just ten more minutes to this shift,

Mimo will again be warned for inattention,

in the air and the rock record

the visible

in the air,

in the rioting motes in the air *in the name of the people*

I command you to disperse, the grain in the air, in the voice.

Half-hearted now the screen proposes other face,

beyond the territory of surveillance, over the fence,

on the patch before the shopping center no shops.

A face from earlier in the day

and other days, from yesterday. The wounded boy

again is squeezed into the space left after the equid is carved,

after the tributes of grain,

after the produce from the mountain are carved.

No lapis is set around the wounded boy.

His body and his face are perfunctory work. Such time

and care as is spent on him is given

to the loving marking of three stylish cracks

through his breast. A body is more than alive,

and life exceeds all bodies, and one way to make sense

of the vacancy there is plexiglas? Cliff in 1986

after the M4 crash: it was only my seatbelt

that kept me from flying through the windscreen.

Beyond the trees the sky now

is wearing a huge dark mask

of cloud and Mimo can sense the seeds of fire inside:

all gathering to burst out

as instant pink tendrils of fire

to illuminate there in the air

the raw wound

waiting to happen again,

pink lines shooting to nightclub

the rest of the day, shooting from open mouth

of grave to coastline of the Lyres of Ur,

buzz buzz as the earth

was scattered ... and it did not

Plastic rock lyric

22.　　Clump of grainy grey dark river flowing round

lighter / is that battery size of paracetamol pulling

face with all blue netting's flagella feeling out

voluptuous to bear rain /　　Go dumb rock record /

ill assembled glacial erratics / so self-similar / like pulling

　　teeth to get solid note from you /　　Sod

summoned back to swamp moisture on top

for a bit / then fire again / wet days we add to ships

while tunes are dry births of this late time / Intent

of bohemian tin / intent of bluestone / intent

of campfire plastic confetti /　　new quality gained

was sharp / composed like persons / but emotions

memories shrieks and ideas still swirled / only congealing

now and then consistency of trifle or imaginary

friend pointing at just how accidental face is /

tide pulling at it all the time / and sky won't stop /

our lamp of love / lone string of pearls / that little feeling

when we touch is still not song / might all still pool

back to oil /　　leading edge subsides

like heavy duty slime /　　Cliff is zone of being

in which condition is also limit / calving to moist /

cultic cave most practical where wound or vein

begs extraction /　　Moisture breezes perish /　　Stone

wobble under headlong finite time, it rock /　　Weather

rushes glass to show / eager glass undecided on

its crystal form just gushes stories /   For plastic

you need climate /   In the beginning was castle

built to weather climate / thence sense of stone

and sand and maternity as Mesopotamian glass bottle

turquoise and dark blue / matter of time

before twelve kinds of copper were seen making

up melody of copper not such river clump of grainy dark /

    I hear you say hello and so want to get to know you

better / learn to make you sing /   Cling like diatoms

cling even to turtles even densely on whales' skin

to this sweet hope / from sugar from liquor

    may we grow friendlier plexiglas to hold us

from the lightning forming fulgurites / the trinitite /

the optic fibre spicules of sponges /   These Apache

tears are hasty melodrama of rock record /   Swim

violent across eyes to make face appear and blur

plastic lighter / stone is already just abstraction

standing short of understanding at sheer mercantile

distance /   try seeing a person as fulgurite, one

glassy conducting spine /   saw it wouldn't work /

    Daily faced by dark vesicular pockets of outer

space in-filled as human form with molten plastic /

try loving a person as lettuce / as thinness of lettuce /

    butterhead iceberg or bibb /   sweet well-watered

lettuce grown in shaded garden of some desert /

all lovely in the beauty of its furrows /   Again

glass intercedes / so ready made for transparency

and shattering / so novel and effacing in its surface

it can't decide which crystal structure to endorse /

has utterly no knowledge interior of dying /

crops springing lively to liquid air /

call for love emerges as

jelly baby wounded boys / Libyan desert glass / trail

from Cornwall and Bohemia to Ur

and dark grey river / I hear you say hello even though

my loving only makes you laugh /   Try to produce floating

sound on flagella / moving fingers

as hummingbird flaps at flower level with no real lingering /

it's only when you tap repeatedly against my forehead

finally these solid sounds sound out of you for grasping

double vision / Plexiglas double vision that comes from no

investment in shattering but sees to how 'adjustable according

to police arm' and 'where you can truly see your loved one

one last time' are two sides of the same sheet

Sea's Hem and Banlieue

23.   On floor of tent the things remaining are arrayed:

witness one flyer from a club in Sheffield, two of Khaled's

buttons, the plastic grotto Zinédine disdained,

phalanx of jelly babies carrying spears of rosemary

and lavender, many various lids, four equids

formed of bread and spit, and a fork. Emael

stop-motions them underwater in their head a film

of exodus through fronds of seaweed, for the reality

of swerve and sway is grounding of the body.

They are sandwich here between sea's hem and banlieue

of woods with pretty much everything they speak

in debt.

       I am cast myself away, they think, an equid

between thumb and index finger, wanting to make

the beginning. Once upon a time … no, hang on,

In beginning was the commotion, yes, and the word for it

was emotion by Emael to Khaled with Zinédine

copied in. Buried like a fossil now in Samsung Galaxy X,

burned out, its crazy surface now a treacherous field

where purple jelly baby fallen bravely herb defences scattered

opens bright to fork. Musing inanely, fires just anywhere,

no surface unconfused and dampness, much, the photographs

keep coming – *the pearling of those waters, the surly punching*

of the fish, her rhythms in the crowd with no rhythm.

                          I am cast myself

down into deep waters away into close fire. I hold their breaths
in severalty but of course will eventually give them up.
Who cannot keep breath must keep tent close to chest.
What is fire? Rain hits my hood, I mean tent, like pebbles
as I am becoming form of the mountain that doesn't exist.
I know myself only as being what struggles or sings or grimaces
or toys with itself in masques.

        The head of an octopus is soft,
very soft, so soft you are at a loss only to have
the grotto, the cultic hard wound begging for extraction,
for processes to start again. Emael's been three weeks in edge
condition now: expose, gnaw, flash, dampness, much, each
tender movement to beginning thwarted: flame confounding blush,
deep water dissimulating tears, visions upwards of innocence
candying with ice.

        What happened E? and how?
Where's all your stuff gone, everything you owed, the jewels,
your dear friends? *The foam that's fringed, the hair that's displayed...*
And the link with this exile, whether internal or external,
can it really be a haggis?
Emael gazes at their wrists and misses
them, the places where Zinédine left hickeys
from his suckers after that hour-long tender hold.
Perhaps he once lived in a bottle of the depths to grow out
of glassy precepts of respect.

So much electric skin amassed,

the images all over them: Zinédine hunching up his shoulders

where there were no shoulders; adding sidebars

to his eyes to make them form of winking

camouflage; the spirit level of his horizontal pupils;

hopping on two arms and waving the others around whenever Jacques

entered the scene; watching rugby bodies on tv together;

doing 'passing cloud' over his skin to show how body is world-

wide and world the very density of body; then the dementia

loop-the-loops before he lifted the lid of his tank that night

to slink off and expire behind the fridge.

Before they smashed the Galaxy, just this message to Mimo

the last one:

🐙

'hey cold bro mine Mimo! How's chops? [*words
stolen sucked away dried up*] It's bad here, hard to
tell. You know that octopus I work with. Found it
dead and dry behind the fridge yesterday. Fuck
me. Everything that holds me with is lacking
skeleton. It steals away through small holes. Soft
Khaled and me we took him to the cove, to lay
him in the deep. It's mad the way his arms. His
breath my breath his breath.   How fast can
you make a fossil Mimo? We scattered sand on
Zinédine. Masked we mounded it. If I was made

of myself I would throw myself away. Fish were nosing and hungry life stirring on seabed so we added rocks and bottles we found and Khaled's bic and my opal ring and some ruby plastic beads. Deep breath   *Flame everywhere, screaming at the turnstiles, welts made by zippers and by buttons, glass blown from windows raining on the street, mountains of glass.* You can't sob when you're underwater but you can dance and you can carve yourself eternal tracery wound into the new rock.   Each thing is a thief and I couldn't take it anymore, breath wouldn't hold to grief so I had to struggle back to surface back to shore embossed in froth. I waited there for Khaled. In mind that octopus fossil, 85 million years old, each arm displayed and the head like a halo around black hole where its ink sack had sunk in. An octopia or a utopus   or some way of taking place once and for all somewhere where each thing is thief. I know Mimo my talents are my debts. You say a person is what takes place when they near plexiglas. What about when that person is part octopus? When I sense my stomach or heart or lung or skin I sense it as another outside. That dull compatible break is what I want to have understood by plexiglas.'

Mimo's response is lost in Emael's shattered phone, under wounded purple jelly baby, scattered herbs

24.   *Scene: Some months before the tent* [Dir.]

On table by the side of their Aunt Ish's bed

in Intensive Care ward these things arrayed:

a bunch of lavender in a glass, a loose photo

of Jacques and Ish against some mountain scene, her glasses,

box of tissues, and Kiki, her little orange plastic octopus.

Emael stilled their heart until their toes were cold,

held their breath, went under deep: they pick up Kiki

and they like the fact this place is called

a unit of *Réanimation*. Ish is struggling.

She's coming back but not to life.

These lanes by cameras in shade of cellphone towers

disguised as palm trees. The garlic when the oil is cold.

Her life is operating outside the awareness

of the unrestrained animal. Parts of her life Emael can see

are distributed explicitly through numbers,

which dwarf the smaller part congealed in smells and memories,

in sensations and the tastes savoured by the orange plastic suckers.

Some of it is in the other beds in other wards.

Don't they know how to hold a skin yet?

Some of it is in a bucket of lights. Emael's sensing

her body is cut with her body; her body is cut

by being this body. The scale of her facets

remains unclear: of housing, of overseas voyage,

of ventilator, of fire?

Maybe always you
have to get burned to touch. What they do know
is that if they keep doing her a Princess cut
they can also keep her fire brilliant.
Like a mother to them, sliding down the slope
igniting trees, erupt by dull edge rubbing
deep down, buzzing sheer rock. For them it is
to help her make it, rescue her from general
condition. Sparkle against tracing. Her cells
and their rage. They will say: inciting contact
probably from Bruno after *manif*, heated nonsense
actual fever, angry at dinner, spitting his fury
at Khaled and at Ish's bright food he said was tasteless,
heaped on salt. 'Women all of you, a fucking coven,
even you Jacques.' And there was Khaled suddenly
turned frozen and untouchable, making his face
an elsewhere, like Zinédine screening 'passing cloud'
show with his skin.

I want you to be near and far
at the same time, Khaled had told E one night
when their holding had been specially intense.
Emael had felt the first signs of frost. Ever since then
their ears would start to scream when only ten feet
down. If they couldn't hold breath under water,

then they'd hold the fucking world under their breath.

But what of this plughole of mouth on the pillow?

The whirlpool swirl of it. Looked to it then

to say the right words, suction of chocolate mousse

the balm again, steady Khaled's skiff, chill Bruno.

Look to it now by nurses clammy in PPE exhausted

through plastic shields, through screen, downspiralling

past grunt in a closed room, every room closed

now under Emael's breath. And if this one true thing

has facets he must cut?

> Of housing?

> *To the tower in the forest.*

> Overseas voyage?

> *My passport, Zinédine behind the fridge, the motor failed.*

> *Mimo overseas, Nin overseas.*

> Of ventilator?

> *Drowned out by breezes.*

> Of fire, then?

> *Her eyes closed, cracks shorter than a mouth,*

Emael trying to hold them to that crack between

what happens and what there is so he can rob it

of its Khaled.

> *Nine days we drifted after the motor failed,*

> *floating somewhere between spirit and shit.*

> *Three days after drinking water finished*

four of us dived into sea to feast on water

and become the sea. Three of us

alive by holding onto keel and mast

we'd lashed together. It was then I saw

each thing is a thief and men are the things

themselves. You must be prepared to eat men.

We got by with short stories, like 'One day

given diamonds, the next day stones'. And one-liners,

like 'A body is transport from border

to border'. No, I don't want to talk about.

Where was the boat of Heaven?

And why is Emael contemplating stealing Kiki

where there was no Emael?

For everyone knows no body

would ever be allowed onto this

Unit of Intensive Care

25.   With Ish gone sad Jacques moped. With restaurant closed

Jacques transparent haunted house, drifted

dragged himself from bed not slept in through to kitchen

where he doesn't eat and television. *Divertissement,*

divertissement-humour, talk show, divertissement,

téléfilm policier. Since there was nothing as it were to keep

the frame propped up the arms and eyelids sank,

and food if there were food, dispersed among the veins,

had same effect as air. Everything held back with her is missing

from the air.

So of course they had to give him some kind

of present. A present tender, with morsels unctuous, tidbit

jewels of snacks, and draughts liquorish. Emael and Khaled

discuss it high on drink and settle on making Jacques

a delicious marriage of their heritages in the form of a Berber

haggis. Back from the halal butcher with bucket of pluck

from a sheep, Emael takes in its mass of lungs and breaks

into the shanty they made up with Zinédine:

O when I lived in a bottle, or so me mamma told me

Take Give Keep Care Hold Well Clear!

I kept my shape as I would gape and let my arms enfold me

Take Give Keep Care Hold Well Clear!

Now rinse your whole pluck in cold water. Trim off

any large pieces of fat and cut away windpipe.

Having plunged in, look at your wrists and hands, how

the brief life they've had in bucket of pluck gives them pink

gauntlets to throw down at lover, laughing, in hope

he'll open up about last night and where there was no

Boat of Heaven. First, ok, let him rouge your cheeks pink.

Let him turmeric your lips and marjoram your ears.

Now place them in a good sized pot and cover with cold water.

The lungs are buoyant so keep submerged with plate

or lid and bring them to the boil. It's hours of simmer,

something rising in them, skimming scum, gestures

to go with song, with pot, breath pledged in divided

draughts. Kiss on eyes like little lamb, kiss deep

with long beak like a bird into plumage. Visionary herbs

and the stench of it rising.

                May the trampled boy steal

breakfast from Director while he sleeps. Kiss love

like a fish on glass tank. All this to feed Jacques, eating

his heart out, bind life back to body, close up the spaces

where images roam unsettling like sharp gobs

of film. Ish in a dish.

              For a while they're concentrated,

grating cooked liver, tossing it with spice, toasting oatmeal,

watching stock reduce. 'We have to stuff this into that',

says Emael at the silence Khaled's doing, staring into meat.

'What are you thinking?' No response.

'I'm sorry, it's not a question I usually ask'.

'I was struck by an image of floating away that fell
in hard showers from the sky. The smaller the pieces
into which you tear a thing, the more you see the colour
dwindling, and smell is not granted to all bodies.
I was thinking of the sea and my part in it. I was thinking
of how when drinking water is finished there are three of us
and objects have no death. Keel and mast – no death.
They are immortal and so bits of god which make the world
mean without end. And that is delicious I thought with Rabbeh –
his name means 'Breeze' though there were no breezes.
And when Aabeh died we tied his body to keel to keep it
from floating away.'

Emael at this point is looking down
at their phone, at Khaled's duckface, Khaled
in his 'Cost of Loving' sweatshirt, Khaled
wearing the jellyfish ring, and then themselves
with Mimo on a Friday chopped with lines of pink light, out
of his head with Nin at her place. Khaled isn't stopping,
images keep striking him:

'Aabeh was tasty like you and softer, younger,
rump like a seal breaching the water.
I meet him in the nights, sometimes from outside
when my mouth is dry, salt on his skin,

and sometimes settling inside me.'

     'Is this a good idea?'

Be aware the filling swells as it cooks so pack quite loosely

into the sheep's stomach when spooning in.

Emael holds the stomach out, murmurs

     'An octopus's head is very soft…'

     'Nothing is so delicious as a keel.

Ever since I learned this I have taught myself to hold my breath

away from me for as long as possible'.

For a while they slowly spoon in the filling,

then Emael pours Khaled another shot of rum, saying

'drink, pretty creature, drink', before breaking again

into song with such a tone that Khaled might almost take

their heart into his own and without knowing

26.   All to give. All to give themselves away. Haggis done,

Emael kept getting flash of Ish with scent of lung,

her head itself a halo on pillow around mouth

black hole where all ink must sink in.

                                    Then Jacques walked in

with eyes terribly remote from each other and an air

of everything having been stolen from him.

Unmasked mouths so weak now and surprising [*fishyface*].

The problem remains how take could ever

have emerged from give, or give from take,

and E has only their drunk instinct of a thief

in flight from catastrophe, checking for cameras,

ducking under laser beams, covering themselves in their path.

        'We made this for you'.

They nod to Khaled, soft. Busy with glasses with knives and forks,

tidy serviceable pride that holds the sacred feast,

the damage, and the *tafn* in one long untraceable line.

Jacques doesn't so much burst into tears, but one does

make its way out, seems to be his, before he wipes it away

to say nothing. The plated haggis also says nothing

but smacks terribly of the Zinédine they found behind the fridge

and Emael feels a touch of what is that anxiety

for wanting this scene to be so jewelled

with its pomegranate, olives, and the cinnamon-dusted cross-sections

of orange like cloisonné of his name: little segment compartments with blazing glass enamel.

Through plate glass in gaslight

ladies laugh at falcons on their wrists, heaped up fruit

and pies and poultry on the heads of goddesses. To work,

this offering needs to be received, the gap in substance

lost from beasts with tears for instance or in perspiration

has to take the form this gift will fit. This for Ish.

But chat which flared up briefly against firewalls,

over deserts, is sputtering in the swamp.

The particles of heat that clumped like pain

or need are flooded and put out.

Khaled is welling up,

and the pomegranate and the olives grey and the fat grey

on the table hunker there, they chill. Jacques' fork still.

'I can't eat this'. He's floundering, Khaled imploring and already

in his queasy belly something half chewed settling:

the madness of this all.

Time for a story.

Emael breathes deep

and glows, tells the first thing that comes to mind:

'So maybe my talents are my debts,

but as any knight of good conscience knows,

that means you can make your disasters delicious, no?

In other words: haggis'.

His face gone accidental,

'I would have been happy with a couscous', says Jacques,
to no one, trembling.

'Oh Jacques, I don't know what to say! It's your friend
Rashid who provided himself this substitute ram for boiled offering.
We wanted just ... to give you something ...'. And Emael at loss
for word shoots an arm out over Khaled's shoulder
as Jacques's shoulder as Zinédine's shoulder
where there was no shoulder.
An octopus's arm is like a human tongue
in mixing radial and longitudinal muscles.

> *That's not a heartbeat, this is*
> *a heartbeat. La da dee, la dee da/*
> *Seven words for gift:*
> *take, give, keep, care, hold, well, clear.*

They take the garnet from their finger, place it on the table.
Unbreathing, they unclasp the startling topaz pig,
it bounces and ends up among the oats and offal.
Silver in the oranges, and gold.
They open buttons on the shirt and scratch a ritual design,
three Bowie flashes on their heaving chest. 'Slap me,
Khaled, hard across the face'.

Khaled frozen beside them
is the slap he doesn't give, and this sting taken
makes no tears, but folds a smirk over their face, a buzz,
a nightclub jubilation disaster. Emael grabs wild at Khaled's ass,

then casts around for puppet, malevolent and unpossessed,

their lighter twitches ready in their hand, for something

that will burn. Buzzing in his ears. Meteoric, yes, they are the one

that is so burning and so all up in the air, an earth-grazing meteor,

or should that be the Boat of Heaven?

'Delicious is the chance you have of keeping

a secret that is visible from the inside but not from outside'.

At this Khaled suddenly stands up ready to go and Jacques as if

operated by the same set of strings can't take it anymore, explodes

in frustration.

'What even are you? What tank did you crawl out of?

If your brother could see you now?

You fucking freak walk out this house now

before you bring its walls and our precarious life

and all it contains now and contained then –

my grief lives here! – and will contain

down with you and my rage

into your swamp. Gather up your scars and…'

With Jacques losing it Emael feels themselves

already an elsewhere. It's because things can be so suspended,

so up in the air, that we evolved lungs. Look at Jacques

there trembling in the strange repetition between each buzz.

Emael thinks a head is only made up of holes:

pupils, nostrils, mouth, ears, all holes, carved portals

for body, with a necklace all that holds complex body

and simple head together.

Yes, when at a quarrelling place

they are figurines brought to life.

'Give me please more holes,

make me all hole' they say silently

inside themselves, and then out loud

to where Khaled had been:

'Why don't you try some of this

delicious orange?'

27.   So that's how Emael ended up in the forest, in that second tent,

a wretched state. This vulnerable shelter, at this point in the novel,

outside Mimo's field of vision, Director lying quartered

in the ward, will stand for the time of speech's intensity.

Olive groves and the hard edge of a general will are hedges failing

endlessly against the wind, against the scale of it.

The ground is warm at day and spiked with dry herb, but gets cold

at night. If not the cocoon of caddisfly supplied with jewels

for its making, then could I at least cast the exoskeleton of myself away

as a cicada? Emael has three of them from daily foragings

in the woods, has arranged them among their findings

at sea's hem that include washed up bottle tops, star fish,

and assorted shells for the grotto. These put them in mind

of childhood digs with Mimo. Prize possession: an owl pellet

they're dissecting to distract themselves, and it's clearly working:

> But now I am a sandwich between sea's hem and banlieue
> *Take Give Keep Care Hold Well Clear!*
> I'll take you for my filling till you've got nothing on ya
> *Take Give Keep Care Hold Well Clear!*

They had hoped to rid these words of the power exercised by objects

which have been the focus of cults – jewels, purple, lapis, flowers,

blood, skin, jellyish textures, blades, sperm, migrants, beaches, tears,

lenses, the digital, crepe, chimeras. But this theft too is futile,

all amps up and struts off back to gift. 'I accumulate rash acts'.
The face of puzzled disappointed Jacques at the end of its tether
latches on to a lizard, darts up a fragrant tree and out of sight.
The owl pellet is soft, ever so soft in harbouring its tiny ribs,
vertebrae, mandible – bare bones of mouse held together
and apart as tangible cloud. What is the arrangement with things
they're trying to arrive at here in this crap stolen tent?
Not that of lone person cult. Remember the time
when they uploaded their selfie for the e-scooter app
which promptly announced: 'Multiple faces recognised'.
Emael feels their body is an intruder that without breaking in
steals the show and will never leave them alone.

Before Khaled soft Khaled cast away melted away got kicked
like a ladder floated away, he had been coming out through
grief, recognising Emael's flesh face in his hands again
after they had fucked things up with Jacques. He began to straighten
the rim of their ear, rolled it, unrolled it, bent it –

'it's getting creased' – then abandoned their ear for cheek –

'I'm making knots in it' –

then eyebrows, chin,

then neck.

It amused him to invent wrinkles.

'You're hurting me'.

'Only a little bit, the eyebrow, just a tiny bit'.

Cut to the beach a few days after that scene: Emael feeling tide of relief and affection coming in, they're keeping an eye out

for a good shell and their arm goes over Khaled's shoulders

only to feel it flinch to something gone.

The particular cast of frown his mouth is doing

has something of plughole or blackhole

to it, and it just kills them.

                        That smoke trickling up from behind

a hill, it must be their smoke, and it's all up to sky, all going

up to sky, and Emael sees as never before that at this moment

they must turn to something else for Khaled's loss to be

no loss but a form of mountain that doesn't exist,

is too beautiful, that holds its nose far from the ground, refuses

to press its lips to the dust or give up on their lava.

They stand outside their own love

like an enemy.

Ignorant of jewels they fasten their jewels round their neck.

Mimo texts innocuous, a buzz, and Emael sends the telephone and

all else out in a fiery arc that causes all light in the land

to disappear.

                'This scene makes Khaled live a moment

in my wretched skin, then cuts him out.' The phone shatters

against the rock beyond the deepest breath. Emael touches now

with fragrant joy the soft bed round the mandible and backbone

they have arranged, not to establish Khaled in happiness,

but that he may emit it. The dig is just the first act to mountain and it's incredible how a good dig takes him back.

In all the caverns are wind and breath, for wind arises

whenever breath is exalted by driving about. When this wind

has grown hot, and has heated all surrounding rocks

by its fury where it touches, and from these has struck up

hot fire with quick flames, it heaves and throws itself up

through mountain's throat and out through the mixing bowl

of its mouth, and so it carries its fire afar and casts itself ash beyond

borders and rolls smoke all fat and fleshy and blurts out gifts

of such wonderful weight you can be certain that this indeed is turbulent

force of breath. And this tremendous event so suddenly gives rise

to parents notified of what is taking place and driving down something

like a motorway too fast in a kind of 1986 so fast

they are wearing no seatbelts and so can fly faster

than any windscreen made of glass.

Two bones of a jaw joint to two tiny auditory bones;

there is a moment yet before the police

clear the scene

Tent / City

28.   Where I once was bound together

with city here on makeshift couch of sighs

I unravel now as palm fibre in this space

divided into left and right atrium,

left and right ventricle, also known as

tent. Animals divided in encampments

of tents because perhaps of their feathers,

by their parts, by how they move,

by how they live, by pools, through passing water

unravelling some will strike tent

hard on bare rock, some on cushion before

warming fast fire over long trees.

As many as have blood

all have a heart, not same heart

or same shape of heart, or same place.

And so hopes come into it, some impossible

to be completed into an animal, but some

at the end of their growth in magnitude become

an egg, of the sort found by Leda,

not unlike a hyacinth, any blue there

betraying hope in sight, in the organs of sight,

which are full not of fire but water.

Rock thrown into wire fence

holds its form in wire fence, and police

is elsewhere, measuring. As many

as have mass and velocity, all are in

the recording, divided in their parts,

the way they move, their lives. He melts

to him, they hold their form in them,

run hard as solitude into wire fence

tent pegs, hard as hope. Not same

the time of generation, by feathers, not same

place. Not only in perception also reason

their abandonment they brought themselves

to this state to the rock the camp they brought

them to the rock they brought themselves

out from the rock to fire they brought their hunger

from themselves and sure enough have heart

attached to windpipes by fatty fibrous

ligatures. Casting from windpipe their breath

often in shouts and yelps and sometimes do a sigh

in the very cold to see a breath and hold its form

as far from themselves as possible to see

that point where an animal, working out a life

of calculations, might hopeful meet a citizen

all by itself and not just by wire fence

or only in perception. We fall to art

of plexiglas, enact some other compatibility

between political, animal, and territorial space,

a compatibility of blue tents hard by

the ring road. Our house was secured on that

painting, with its payments: fastened by ferret

the thought of my heart. If this art

brings house to tent, if you spunk

up the structures you have no actual

house to speak of, if your blood is also

the salt water your roof slate gray sky. Whose

warm dream place of fire licks olive grove,

licks paintwards, spunks crossbeam not

my actual house. The world under the skies

is changed. For every animal with blood

who takes air from outside, the aqualung hotel

the scuba same but not in the same place,

from necessity has length measured out

in copper stripped from wiring boxes.

And from the changing skies comes storm

covering like a tent this field of living

with a beating sound like wings making the point

that neither our tame nor pale,

neither our rock nor fire

is a difference of winged

but drives home some holding facility made personal.

And so they pipe from windpipe breath

in storm to show where speech might be

and arms waving and the next thing is to speak

about the cause of these sorts of monsters
as seen in the mortgage painting, for in the end
when the movements including the rocks
and spunk and crossbeaming are not mastered
the movements slacken and what is most of all
particular is left.

                Can we talk later heart
not in this? We can make new rocks now directly
from all dirty breath, from all storm, from
tear gas, tiger moth, the cry of pre-world owl.
But tent pegs. Loving murmurs in her rosy arms
to reach the edges of the earth. Heart
not over this, tent pegs out. Draw close the shining
tent flaps, leave them babble endlessly, when
each time a rib buckles we are provided
with a click. Arid beetle off police radar
tymbal deck itself in substance
not itself, extrude its own shine, gold and turquoise.
Let these then be the causes of the differences
in eyes so we do not speak of a fish having a face;
we speak of its two faces having a fish.
We speak not of the tent being 40% children;
we speak of all these larvae-like things having emerged
in cells like bees and see that bees
should come to be out and about

even if not brought about by bees.

We speak of how only the ferret looks right

in the painting and of our tent's semilunar valve

flapping to the storm

See You Through

29.   So this is what there is for work for Mimo now, for me?

This nonsense, these different forms of blank?

Yesterday, the crudeness of the algorithm,

a linear construction lining up the data from the BBC,

the bingo clubs, the legal aid boards, banks,

the NHS, estate agents, the swiping

of medical cards, and Mimo asked to drop in,

to confirm, a set of CCTV images that signal error.

His role to drop the image in the pattern,

agree it was a face,

                    not wrong face,

then let the statement stand and pass on to the DWP.

Yesterday that horror of naïve approval. Today the pig.

Be sure to read through this literature bundle to familiarise
yourself.

            And he has. Who writes this shit? 'Pig face includes
pig's eyes, pig's nose, pig's ears, and other biological
features'. 'Convolutional neural network' recognition used
that's been 'trained up' with large numbers of 640 x 480 pixel
images doctored by 'enhancement operations such as rotation,
translation, hue, brightness, shading, scaling, and adding salt
and pepper noise disturbance'. 'Training our network
over 500 epochs takes approximately 5 minutes'.
'We did not deliberately ask the pig's face to be clean
so as to obtain a clean and dirty pigface pictures'. Fuck's sake.

And what have they ended up with? 94%
recognition success with it for all the sample pigs
except one that's rocking 36%. That mass of prancey
pallour, form already dotted through with lines
marking picnic shoulder cuts, belly bacon,
tenderloin. You can't get jewel from pig, can't facet pig.
What point to pig individual? Pig crowd
together against form. Pig clump
not riot. Dear little pigsney has mamma's mouth,
lipstick on a block of pig iron, not even dignity
of unit, pigbed. Snout. Pignut. What point
to pig evasive? Who wants to wrestle
the idea of a single special pigface
back to mittelmass? Pig clump not riot.

Watch the feed, we need to know why Pig 17 is only 36%
recognisable, otherwise the whole software is just a disaster
waiting to happen.

Ha, there he is, and yes
he sure has a swagger unlike the other pigs,
as though he's found the line between what there is
and what happens and is corkscrewing about the pen
not so much making himself visible as imposing presence,
a swervy curvy manifold mass that's covered
any amount of himself in mud and shit to point
he's raised himself up to level of generic pig,

and more than that:

an average character of raw material.

Mimo's head is shaking here, proud in a way of this lump

and its evasive smiling squeal through all the rules

applied to surface forms, to figures and to faces.

But Emael is miles away, a week now with no news, and Jacques

not answering, Khaled entirely disconnected, and the graven

weight of some of the people not pigs in that job

from yesterday now losing benefits, cast aside. You cut

the image in the copper plate but pig

gives no margin, all the space is flattened out with pig.

When captured, pig won't live apart from screen,

bristle pixel pig.

Dürer had no intention ever

of engraving pigs before those most beautiful huts.

A large horse, yes, a small horse, something

allegorical and many kinds of dogs, but just imagine

how little Dürer wanted pigs: make me as one

of thy hired servants. Unable to say it,

he spent the whole day roaming around outside,

didn't even want to have the dogs with him

because they too loved him, because in their presence

he could do nothing without giving pleasure or pain. Pigs,

the answer came and fortified the plate,

no margin, nothing but plate. But one piglet

in the foreground is only 36% in the image plane

shared by the rest. O now look at him go!

A little mincey at the back and butching it up front

and the effect on main body is a swervy

undulating coasting-it not unlike a great white shark's

while tail is held up like a tiny paper parasol

in a cocktail, and head is both nodding a bit

and shaking a bit simultaneously like the action

of reading, and it's as if all motion

is always one long chain and new motion

arises out of the general, and clearly first beginnings

have made by swerving a beginning of motion

such as to break any decrees of fate

by which we proceed where pleasure takes

each in the form of this pig. In other words:

body first to body out; pig first to pig out.

Against himself, Mimo flows out with this ever-emergent pig,

whose wild smile and utter degradation is for him alone.

Keep it close. Detection of absence of pain

is hard to code, but when you let pig into city,

what's the point in trying to render fortifications?

What you pignorate today will never be redeemed.

No place not full of trampled, prime cuts, cheap cuts.

Prime smile. And are those four tiny diamante boots

and a magenta feather boa not visible

so much as a salt and pepper presence imposed?

And if he is an average character of raw material

does he know it without seeing it like a Tiresias, or

does he do it without knowing it like a genius?

Clearly it falls on Mimo to see to his realization

of the unspeakable: any such character

also must be seen as figure of the Gross Domestic.

He sets his eye to a kind of free indirect piggybacking

as form of looking on:

> *She sat down again and resumed her work, a crocheted*
>
> *orange octopus. She worked with her head lowered,*
>
> *nodding and shaking simultaneously. She did not speak.*
>
> *Neither did Jacques. Little breezes blew beneath the door*
>
> *and eddied dust over the tiles, and he watched it swirl*
>
> *about. He could hear nothing but the throbbing inside*
>
> *his head and the squeal of a pig somewhere away*
>
> *in the farmyard.*

A kind of blanched out love in no form settles, colour

drained from jelly slabs, movement stilled from nightclub,

riot taken out of riot, pig clump white meat soldier,

pure feed, shields formed to that police arm

melt into necessary accommodation of any war.

Set tub of lard on kettle on slab on kettle on keg

of butter, onions, fish forms or octopus or particular tender

hold on just that soft flesh, boil down to general meat

white meat. What there is for work for Mimo,

no more work for Mimo.

He will not give this face,

not give that erroneous pig face,

not give face to trampled boy.

So what was the problem with Pig 17?

You tell me. It's just your average pig.

30.   If there is one thing his father tried to instill in him

is a disgrace. Less a matter of paternity

than of patterning, embellished with proverbs.

Mimo sees him now walking off from them oddly h

disappears, then reappears from a station toilet,

buys a newspaper to hold the world at arms' length

behind its news in hot train carriage, Emael and Mi

sitting opposite him. Is that dirty breath? No, it's sm

gathering and spreading from their father who's hav

reading nonchalant.

What has been destroyed is property

of the gods; no one can take it away.

Mimo can neith

nor locate the smell of that destruction. All things are

seeds and a fixed parent, and it seeps out when he trie

the gods or melt employment in a fire. Today, for exan

half wild from turning down the contract for the DWP

on saying 'no' four times to the Director, not just signin

but actually powering down the workstation, Mimo tur

to LammasLand and breathed his liberation deep and \

came the stench of pattern, alien matter cast out

from matter on the ground, things with bodies fleeing b

I don't work for you.

But the story's just beginning. At this po

in the plot there are reckonings.

Mimo reckons the Director
is in and out of consciousness with some ventilator
doing his breathing, his reanimation, his inspiration,
his show of 'character'.

I mean now that you've touched on paternity
where's the father been in all this?

Paternity in its fluid state,
or labour, creates value but is not itself value.
It becomes value in its smelt or coagulated state
as form of gold. The value of paternity as a congealed mass
of human pattern can only be expressed with proverbs or allegory
as materially different from any human and yet common to
that human and all others.

Gliding on down the street's middle
to avoid masked passers left and right Mimo feels himself
sandwiched between the shops' panes, a creature hard at himself
for where to turn. Finally he swims towards the light
of a *Pret a Manger* – fuck's sake, he thinks, as another proverb
comes to mind:

If the lion heats the soup, who would say
it is no good?

Only wait, soon, he thinks, you too will rest.
He is weary of dictated activity, wants much less theme
and more polymerization. He's leaning to the utopia
of what is close at hand, a ham sandwich and some crisps,

but breath of distance is borne in front of these images,

he's in danger just of recognizing their faces too,

just separate existence, breath from the Director sick

in reanimation ward, in every sickbed, virus in him, close

to coma. *Plow it under by gold.* Director is neither holding

breath nor breathing bodies out from deep beneath

by weary pants. Director is imperial translation, all connections

broken, so the message clumps into a single pathway.

Director broadcasts to Mimo through the clinic sewage system,

through the drainage and the porous walls.

When your father mother

died, when the car crash, when Emael laughing lit your cheeks?

When you watched as Emael...

Green tent. Green brackets.

Green as Emael lit the match to light the fire to burn

their combined childhood ages, nine plus seven,

into a green sheet of play glass; the materials to make it with

at hand, beach sand, bbq ash, jelly babies, and eucalyptus

leaves, and the dry wood so childishly enthusiastic

with its flames, and the enthusiasm so infectious, passing

to dry grass and now to trees and Emael jumping about

beside themselves volcanic all with joy.

Mimo is out of work

completely in this remembrance at last for a second,

utterly superfluous to Emael's incandescence,

recognizing nothing. He's finding finally a way to make the animals

come near us and place them on the ground, on the floor

of the world at the very moment 'world' is destroyed.

And Emael and the jelly babies fighting still to stay upright

in the scene so they can see what's going on, can take it

in. This tender vacation, burning on the far side of scarcity,

is short: of course their parents were called up to be immediate,

to be emergency, the glass form of their mother already

trembling at breaking point in the car beside their father

whose tendency to be always fighting us off elsewhere

as money made him just the right mercenary for the scene.

      Yes, right: character! Once upon a time, the grieving children

dash a plaster mask against a pillar or a beam

and have expressions now to work with. Your creature is confirmed

by damage! Something for your pocket, track of crumbs ...

Roads stretch to edge of the severalty and sky

also is full of roads. Each road sequences a stream of speeding cars,

and no road leads beyond the tent, and this is pictured

as happening in public.

The damage must be great.

31.　　Director in the clinic objecting to the graph, his monitors,

the tedious breathing going through him.

Care locates Director in his body,

and his fever and his eyes shut and his no taste

no smell no oxygen in blood no consciousness

to speak of strain against that limitation.

He's trying to get through, he must island

Mimo in a pool of viscous panic,

pouring fast enough to keep him raking spill back

to his given limits for eternity. Director

broadcasts from his dreams four great columns of blood descending.

The first falls most furiously and inundates all the countryside,

with such a crash it wakes Director in the dream,

so when the other columns topple, fall from such height,

having no dream to contain them, they seem to fall slowly.

Mimo surplus to this dream is blasted yet

by wind and flying spray from random passing car

that carries smell of pattern smell of shit

with residue of voice.

　　　　　　　　A heart which knows no accounting,

is it a wise heart? Father up!

　　　　　　　　　　　A human pattern can wait

for eighteen years hanging from the end of a streetlight, waiting

paternal. When a human passes under this pattern's

lookout post it drops down. It is fishy butter whiff

of affection emanating from the human's apocrine glands

that guides the pattern. When fallen onto the human,

pattern attaches itself; temperature of blood keeps

pattern burying there to suck blood of affection,

and only at the moment when the human's blood

enters into pattern's stomach do pattern's eggs open,

mature, and develop, establishing a tax

on every several face.

      Loss of my owned

making, rounding a corner with my sandwich

watching its edges bearing their distance before them.

   The plough furrows the land

but the camera defends the land. Let everyone who can smite,

slay and stab, secretly or openly.

      And woah!

  'Jason Donovan, wow, it's really … I can't believe it. Step back in

  time: I had your duet with Kylie, 'Especially for You', in my head

  just this morning!'

  'Piss off, wanker'

  'What?! No need to be like that… I was just expressing …

  welcome surprise or something…'

  '___'

Why would he be like that? Mimo turns to phone. 'For Christmas,

Donovan was due to make his pantomime debut as The Evil Ringmaster

in *Goldilocks and the Three Bears* at the Birmingham Hippodrome, however due to COVID-19 pandemic the panto has been postponed

to next year'. Hm. Maybe wasn't Jason. Maybe it was Disaffection.

Disaffection is walking head down across the street.

Disaffection's jeans are too tight on old calves.

Disaffection now is staring in a shop window

pretending to look at handbags hoping to space out.

Mimo's startled by the rebuff and the change

of frame, and tickled slightly too: he'll follow

white meat plump shank with no screen

and no grid to click to. Something throbbing

ticking in him now. To this practical apprenticeship

in the development of relation he adds the crow

that's lighted on the car across the road

and is honing its beak on the rear-view

mirror. He knows it as *Post Scarcity*. Post scarcity

is learning something vertical by heart, learning without repetition,

secure as a nest. A nest not my actual house,

not my actual tent, suspended with branching, open to moss

and wiring and blue netting over a field of living, as nest of identification

on the scale of a great mountain firmly grounded,

its insides resounding with song, its exterior the sky,

and the breezes in its corridors sweet as the voice

of a calf, continuous in air, eye, ear, lungs, wings, and nerves.

Post scarcity is jaunty and has hidden

pieces from the bright parts of a pigeon

in the guttering of several houses. Mimo in the street

is still spattered with Director [*normality is one intentional product*

of the interaction with work. Work is the activity that confronts

what is missing from the organization of work] but Director is resounding

as brass for Mimo. In his tubes and his fluids and his Gantt charts,

strange times when a prince can win heaven

with bloodshed better than other men with prayer.

     A rebel is a man who runs,

               and Mimo jaunty in the air

runs out and over a field of living

32. Emael, Emael, wherefore art thou? How many days

has it been since last in touch? I feel your presence

by touching that wall and as I touch that wall

I feel your blood. Not together I move my arms palms

to wall as wings and then outside I am outside

with clumps of grass so green too much like oil

burning on horizon where the sound of sucking hookah-

pipe on terrace might be sound of distant machine-

gun fire. My wings and these clouds of acrid, the close

suck and sluice of what we take inside us mutually to mix

with sluice of blood and other waters there already.

And the noise of distance, pointed reminder

of my pattern built from outside – word in my ear –

bearing distance before it as it burrows in to find the shape

that must receive it. Digging channels there and building

forest, tents and green light, spine, a beautiful lake

from which theory mists up as you rest by it.

What can a peasant see in a lake of beauty?

      A peasant has to drink the whole lake, set the lake

on fire, or slowly add her own disintegration to the organic

matter turning the lake murky green. Beauty

comes to peasant only by message by balloon

drifting past the walls and army, only by carrion pigeon

freed to pause and taste of herbs by the lake.

Do they sell tarragon at Aldi? A crow up on its gutter,

maybe done with its last bright part

of pigeon. Is the eating of one species by another

really the simplest form of luxury? And is eating death

in accidental form really the height of luxury?

Mimo recalls those glasses in development

he had to trial, what were they called?

VisionTaste. Like Google Glass, but focused

on an 'elite clientele' wanting to buy art and luxury

objects: evaluations flashed up in RealTime with 'universal

voice' of emojis, the Premium service calling

on a networked sweatshop of peasants trawling

the web. He knows that memory still in his retina;

sometimes when he looks with love

on the sheen of a crow there burns

the hint of a green bracket, a match

with a handbag, a large number,

an enormous network. These whitemeat moments

of pig rump suffering out of species, inefficient wings.

The glance of a noise from the tree above him, its beak

nuzzling a woodlouse in his ear for later, the crow speaks

disappointment in this iteration. The crow is angry

about being in a novel. The crow's vision is rattled

with yellow plastic bags and being held to realism.

Our beaks are too clumsy in this book to build an image.

You have numbered the branches and the loose wires,

and any crow can see that there are not enough to build

a model of the landscapes of our dreams. A plummet

through thin air to land tense standoff on the ground,

hop claw hop,

still the disaster of the cracked shell, where your light

pours in. We make this from moss. We track the grubs

on the ground of the sun and the grubs within spring ground,

they clad themselves with turquoises, with short rods

of gold. Fashion this with stop motion of Waitrose bags.

Mimo deflates as the balloons bearing Emael messages
of beauty deflate. Lost of my own making.

How to keep up
with their branching, stay open to moss, wiring, field
of living. The crow calls him back to being before the Standard
of Ur in the British Museum gazing at its panelled War
of naked bodies, wounded boy, chariots, and equids,
and its panelled Peace of feasting with lyre. VisionTaste
flashed up face-without-mouth plus scream-face
emojis – clueless – and then Premium voice
from the sweatshop in his ear-piece asking *where exactly*
are you?

But now he's seeing the Standard better,
the War panels' patterning bearing him very different voice
to coagulate with:

bad news from home, in the form of tin, on the whole,

over the top, those lungs of yours, someone

in arms against, a one-in-five risk,

tabled, already filled, a place burning over your head,

framed, cast, having shot

a man, turning from a woman, every inch, beating

mind, a spy hunt, holding a line, suspended

absence, the names of the killed.

Death in accidental form, death in short shorts,

when the music stops, through curved plastic,

or death dripsplashed in plastic

melted from the ceiling, by miracle of beak

in time beyond work, arranged just after the beat

within a faceted limestone frame in tiny pieces

of windscreen, large dull plates of plexiglas

glowing in pink laser

33.   With more free time, Mimo's helping out his friend.

Only three of the pale kids with their sunk eyes

and salt-stained patina have actually surfaced

for the session. Nin's unsurprised, beyond surprise

these days. She's made a call to the Department,

so someone will look into it, trawl along the front for strays,

get to them she hopes before the police do.

                                        Mimo

is feeling gloriously available. Something gave,

he has forgotten sheets of plastic visibility

today is glory and no work to perform, is balanced

high above a sump he screens out. He's helping out his friend,

he's making time for troubled youth – his free steps

compact plastic ground, voices sweet herb fragrant rising

with his tread. 'Writing workshop' doesn't seem right.

It was down at the sea front that the phrase 'novel acoustic

imaging' came to him again, he was staring out

at the sheepless field of sea dancing its oblivion

over the largest mapped medieval underwater site in Europe

and he'd thought of setting them to write

of any sea creature they like.

                            Nin in such a bad way

drinking like a fish now and it also seemed a way of holding

Emael close with no word from them.

                                    I can't tell you

how much I want to keep you close.

'Whatever you want',

he tells them, looking at the three of them, each not unique

but of a number numberless. Maybe a shark,

a whale, a crab that scuttles sideways. Just get inside it

for a while and tell me what you see or what you feel

or what you find. They aren't even laughing at him,

they are centuries underground their tombs and equids

and their lapis lazuli. Then Grace meets Trebor's eye

and Trebor compacts silently with Chehon

and the room gives place to scaly creatures as they open up

a liquid path. Their heads are down – occasionally

they'll go to the computer to check a fact, but mostly

there is silence and mouth breathing and the words of creatures

of the sea. Chehon's found the voice of Octopus

becoming fossil, and will write something like

I feel the press of plastic

bottle and an opal ring and sand, and time, and of the grief

at last of those two breathless beautiful,

and my softness that had flowed in always

where my vision led grows compact

with the rock grew compact.

Yes, that's right,

such big young love is terribly hard and tender

and cruel, calls up that gift Emael had in mind

of glass green its fragments to be made into some ring

so delicious the giving of it would be a devastation

pure devastation without return like a form of parent

all to give. The thing, Mimo had told them,

is to find a voice that is *over* your voice. Something not a dream

is occurring to Grace, who settled on a clownfish:

Fiction,

it is true, thrives on substitution in the love relationship.

As when your mother dies your father should have changed

sex to take her place.

Maybe think the writing is a tent or

an aquarium or a cave for you to find things in? Maybe

someone left them there for you? In his lost city

ravaged Trebor scrabbles stickleback with bloody knuckles

in the rough sand, secreting something from kidneys

through his cloaca, body hunched over his nest.

Under the stairs

in the mall and in the marshes of Ur

I layer algae with sand with stuff

I find and then you try to take it from me,

even when I glue it with my guts

in Doggerland you watch me

and you want to take it from me.

And so it is that Trebor

made his face a kind of rock face as to say

Sump this!

See, you can't

but Mimo knows it fragile

like the exoskeleton Emael left him with when Emael got taken

away. Body first to body out. Then submerge to merge.

Trebor's stickleback makes live character

of scars. Voice on voice. Over voice. Mimo is thinking

of the pipefish that piggyback on vegetarian parrotfish

to hide from prey before they glide down

swallow them down speechless. So when he speaks,

Chehon's voice already has an opening

to hold to.

What's that thing they've got?

The black thing making circle stain on rock

here? Is it in my head? I know my brain

is everywhere – I've marked it on my arms look

with these sigla.

Mimo's dug a mine

under these words. The subland children chatter

forth and back in endless give:

what if the stickleback

learns sumptuary destruction? Remember how tiny your father

was for so long until he suddenly had to grow

into a mother? Arms! – not tentacles! How long

can you fishface at a mirror before you kiss yourself?

Or he is running on a roof ridge reconstructed

from fragments found scattered by tides and trawling.

Mimo's tuning in, but images of sound that try to capture

epochs are shit for actual several fish. Grace's face

is sending tears out silent across its frozen landscape

and then she unleashes a short angry scream

as form of mirror. Mimo blushes.

To descend

> *through the darkness to grace them / till darkness*

were lovelier than light.

Nin is struggling, has just done a silent belch

beside Mimo that smells awfully like someone else.

'You're doing really well with this', she tells them,

'just keep playing with it till it's sound'. Silence,

so Mimo asks, 'Novel acoustic imaging,

what does that make you think of?' and Grace replies.

The lamentation

is the depth of the boat.

Nin is moved to say

'Oh that's great, you have to keep holding on to insights

like that'. Grace folds her arms. 'Keep holding on?

sounds like that shit ginger singer my dad ...'

– terrible tender

hard and cruel are adolescents

34.   Oh dear, Nin's not taken that well, is doing a smile

but its tightening centre is more a form of plughole

for her face to swirl down. Mimo feels her embarassment

and makes a window by turning to gaze out of it.

Are those doodles she's scored on her blank pad?

More just a set of scratches. Three slashes, three wounds,

what to make of them? A not-equals sign? A hut?

A mouth? Mimo is half way to pity or contempt,

sees himself fold Nin's discomposing face in green brackets

and launch the habitual mechanism,

but the pale children fire up strange with her.

Smashing him, their wounds open, for her gift

imposed time. Chehon slashes three times too

on his page, then writes

> *a strata isn't like a phase,*
> *this gesture caught compressed is holding your world up.*
> *Rock of my trampled stain, rock of my flexibility, stone*
> *of all the body follows anywhere my eye can go, adamant*
> *taste of your jewels to that boy's soft scared skin.*

                           Mimo feels his skin

prickle up a wave of panic over him. Emael.

Yes, that's how life is taken, for this gesture caught flying

through a window, flying through a windscreen, is not

just your own but is tangled with others as flagella. Chehon

composing frantic inside Mimo's panic lays down

rock on me, not only glass and crystal and crude
forming under my pressure from your discarded,
but fine river sand on me and water you did not
dive into.

Warm and puzzled in her state Nin enthuses
'Smashing it!' Trebor gutsy feels it pass to him, and Mimo's eyes
flick fast from one to other

dried fish is simply
exchanged for jellied birds, with no stipulation,
but try cementing joy to my nest? –
its breath pursues me as it rushes to the forest.

Jeweller of rock, gaoler
of gesture. Simply, simply … what?
To put it simply, they robbed me of my unlived life's best
gestures, they had my joy and baths
of action more than me, and so you have to make up
parental story to make out some plot behind it, no?
'Trebor, seeing as you're dwelling
inside stickleback nest, what do you make
of inner voice?'

The miracle of inner voice is this reciprocal
penetration of detachment and intimacy, lone soul
and the social … The chorus floats inside, fills the space,
and this happening does not set itself apart;

we do not remain just witnessing ... Mystery –

something fictional and not representational –

I compare to plexiglas.

Emael in the tent they made me

be a tree and laid my grief before them as mosaic of soft jelly

sweet and giggled it and kissed and wept.

Emael in the club my ecstasy so bright in them my dancing

legs gave way and nothing in the breathless mirror gave me

back. The crown fused to my head and parent stuck

like ivy. Grace, absorbed,

the mucus and the toxin,

and the bath of sound, and then the rush

to the locked gates,

and the intensity of flame.

Every word in all language is gift,

and in no world are give and take two different gestures,

but the nexum springs from things as much as people,

the wounded boy, stripped and lashed,

has stepped out from behind the screen.

Grace, amused, *just because it's orange!*

Another special belch from Nin, so Mimo asks Grace

'The voice? The voice is orange?'

Why not? For a voice

is scattered abroad in all directions, since voices engender

other tones of voice when one voice uttered has leapt

several to many, just as a cinder is accustomed to throw

itself into making other fires of its own. And so places

hidden away from sight are teeming with voices,

and all boil and stir around with sound.

Mimo's arm is confused
about the room it is in. Water rushing through, fish
borne joyful on the rush, plastic seaweed and fine river sand.
He tries to press himself against the glass, there is
no glass, he stumbles in a little pooling dance
of care. This is not work. Grace giggles at herself;
Chehon snorts; Trebor buzz buzz to announce the general
spillage. There is no measure to his making, no place
for so many different kinds of fish in Mimo's narrative arc.
He is out of the picture. He wears a wrap of heavy light
and resin, poured from three slashed wounds, unrecognizable,
the equids bearing tributes in another frame, and everything
is looted from him save this care stretching out
to adolescence.

What is the one word that a child needs
most?

That's right, *No*. And what were the two words
that Emael first held tight? *Yes* and *More*. In other words:
recipe for disaster. They have taken my best life,
and I love them for this crime, I love them in this voice.
And if I've had to pool a little dance for that, well,
it must have been a disco inferno

15 Criteria for Novel Gestures

35.   **15 Criteria for Novel Gestures**

A parting gift – pure devastation without return – for the Director

1. They are made so acquaintances might drink together, so foreigners might cruise about as new fish, so those bathed for holidays might rejoice in public squares.

2. They take the pluck of some unlived life and make a haggis.

3. They aren't *for* you: a pig in an aquarium can only be sustained if no one tries pulling its actual face. Any allegory levering itself up on pig rump through the word 'crisp' is neither here nor there.

4. They make live second-hand jewels of what lies around the corner.

5. The police clear the scene; they encounter the police.

6. They install plexiglas with inner voice so style is indeed at least two persons.

7. They are mechanically ineffective (i.e. don't directly catch prey); can't even work out how to remove their new garnet ring for the MRI scan.

8. Those who find them inelegant or hard to believe should check a recent screenshot of themselves and give in to abjection, jubilation, euphoria, melancholy, devastation, aggression, and a leap into collectivity.

9. It ain't easy being pretty and it ain't pretty being easy, so they do care in the hardest ink.

10. While sketching the fate of brickwork, they keep believing in a nest, a tent, a hut, a boat as means of living on the crack between what happens and what there is.

11. The price of them; it makes you dim the screen.

12. They hold no assumption but holes for the mooring-poles of heaven.

13. Parent is always a feint – pointing you on and through the broken windshield to mosaic, then on and through mosaic to fine river sand.

14. They are hesitant to name equids 'horses', when most of them are still so tiny and their destiny is not yet established.

15. Emael has thieved the best of them.

Take Give Keep Care Hold Well Clear

36.   Emael and their tent are pitched beyond surveillance.

While the water in the end will claim the land

they pegged it to, the sea will not know they were

there. While the police will clear this camp, consume

this forest, turn them and others like them face

to concrete wall, will spray gases in their face,

trample their shrine; police do not know that this is Emael,

that Emael is here. Emael is pretty sure of where,

but not of when; it's like because they've not spoken

to Mimo, Mimo is making himself a high-pitched

presence or a kind of tone in Emael. Mimo, so deadset

on his flat's brickwork, on gauging the world

by stroking its walls, is in this tent a fear of its flappy here-

and-now as some future what-if in which no ink

will sink no breath will draw. Neither here

nor there, another botched job. But what if Zac Efron's

new jaw and his wild new face are just correction

finally of damage from the accident

in 2013? All the care in Twitter rushes in to cushion

Zac against suspicion of filler and a clumsy procedure:

we are all seeing that chin in the glass now.

Is this what it is to be together?

Enormous love pours terrifying violent through

those tiny holes. I can do Mimo's thoughts on it here:

the face

in the glass forces me to turn and face it,

which is under sentence of death.

And I can't tell what moves in this face,

from this face...

And that is because while Mimo has the face
of an imminent accident, I have the force
of an imminent accident.

Take 2: no glass,
but Mimo staring open-mouthed through his plexiglas
tank of gaping fish at me on the other side air-kissing
dreamily at some beloved who isn't here. Identity
is theft. Better to have loved and lost
than never to have lost at all.

Take 3: Mimo flicking through
every face in every database to find a match for the self-
restoring immediacy of the trampled boy, a holiday
out of work. He's willing to life the phone thrown
at the base of the cliff and shattered, when it hit the rock
gorilla glass shattered Cliff not shattered but glorious
in his plexiglas tank. Flicking through the faces in the database,
even through the pigs, dirty pigs and pigs with clean faces
and the single pig so average it has no image, Barry Gibbs
sings unconsoled.

It rides unrecognised
on such enormous love. I carry that boy's heart

like a full bucket picked up in the dark.

The images I make myself he doesn't see are images to give

some life not taken. The sense after the five

is sense of what-if and could-have-

been, and its organs are stomach and lungs.

                                                    Last night,

neither here nor there, so drunk and stoned

on images my stomach spinning out with eyes

closed on one vision of black towering column without

end or outline and I span it and gave it to the earth

and watched a crow feed on it break of day.

'Post scarcity' is what Mimo would call it, his airs whistling

through the leaking mitral valve in the tent, condensing

and hardening on fine walls of the artery that leads up

past the ear and disappears into the mind, dimming

against the incredible scale of love. In time everything

is believable, and in space everything

is breathable. I'm so far from him that he can almost

touch me.

37. Sunlight through my fingers' webbing, brings back

the dancefloor's scanning high-pink cone of smoke

the first time I felt myself able to take on different scales

of the mountain that doesn't exist but might –

only to see Mimo watching me and resolving to make himself

my disaster where there was no disaster. Images

can stream through glass and warmth trickle through

silver. Emael dirty hand a scent of rosemary

and lavender from tent floor passes down my thigh

and gently scabs the knee. Twitch and glide are latent there:

on the dancefloor my glory jumped the music

to new hosts, they pass in droplets of light

and through the very air. Emael in the nightclub

is a bait ball of dense promise,

dancers nip themselves and others in the mirrors

and the space they open. They flame

and flame. And Mimo, there he is hard spine

trying to pool a little of the dance but in the face

of all this coming to an end like a carp

in deep waters where he just can't take the promise

or the space they open. A crime. Making himself

my disaster also made a secret of me

to keep me safe and party to himself. A secret

always makes three: a guardian, a witness, and the excluded.

He quarantined. He aquariumed, his building falsely

and his perishing truly: little bother me in disco frenzy

breathing under homeless banner.

In wrath and terror and in masks, in all the faces

recognized, the silting of the outlet to the gulf.

My heads lay scattered, and dancing bodies ignorant

of silver filled their hands with my silver. To look at him,

you'd have thought he was just separating

a harvest's good grain from the bad,

and then his comfort in this becoming

way to take pleasure in structures of setting-aside:

restroom facilities, hidden drawers, piggybank,

mirrors, fishtank, 'office', so I might keep cropping

up all over the place? The pattern

seemed obvious. 'Mimo', I'd say, 'remember

the old proverb: "A donkey eating its own bedding

ends up taking everything personally"'.

His reply: 'What if we only identify by losing some body

each time?' How can I keep cropping up,

when every flare settles by the turnstiles

as a mass of melted plastics, saddening the police

a little, cheap provincial brands? How far back

and how high up would we need to be

to give this sprawl into a story? I'll surely have to be

left out, to be turned out of time.

Were Mimo here was this exchange?:

Mimo, have you looked in the drawer again?

I have.

How does it fare?

Good.

Have you looked in the fishtank again?

I have.

How does it fare?

All for your good.

Have you looked in the mirror again?

I have.

How does it fare?

For good.

Did you work with the piggybank again?

I did.

Good for you. What kind of work?

Detective work.

Emael is brought to tears of frustrated structure

like spilled dry paint like three carved scars

on a trampled boy, as Mimo's beneficent retention

– he holds these truths to be good! – sprawls out

in their memory on their broken

phone, laments over territory deep

enclosed for breath. They were set out

for elsewhere and arrive elsewhen,

here at sea's hem, the burning nightspot, Ur.

The monogram of autumn signs itself,

an isolated plant of high-pink owl-head clover

under the kind of tree whose shade is so grave

it aches the head who lies in it.

Mimo's secret is he has become all three:

guardian, witness, and excluded in his interior

he can't wholly enter or leave. Were Mimo here

was this to sound a resolution?:

> *Life is not an I*
>
> *or even our existence. It is as buried as 'octopus'*
>
> *as it is concealed as 'well' or 'sump'.*

                They gather themselves

to pass out from heart of tent to head

towards the shore, all abuzz

as they swerve themselves motions beginning

38.   Striking tent to past tense, trusting parts of what I kept

into small deep burrows (jelly babies, fork, defunct Galaxy)

and other parts of my possession to burn in time and fly

up as a kite, I make my way from left hip to right hip,

spine swerves as path curves down from woodland to the sea.

Grateful decorations to my ankle from small thorns

and other plants that lash, and from the perfume

this south keeps close down to earth. Sometimes made my way

down when the lift was broken in the tower

down back steps fragrant also, decorated with love

past graffiti: 'KHALED IS FULL OF INCLUSIONS'; 'PRINCESS

WILL CUT YOU'. Deep breath.

                              Yes, waking again up to no one

this morning:

        I will see through my delight, I will see

through your cold hands on my warm back.

                              Then staring

at the ants in grass swarming to biscuit crumbs and thinking

a child takes infinite care to lift the patterned wallpaper,

scrape out the plaster behind, and then place within the hollow

the treasured object before pasting paper back so perfectly

that nothing happened and by this procedure their life

is secreted safely away. Second hand smooth down wall

like bedsheet smoothed on sleep, while coast of inner

life is open to the waves, a large bear with violet gums

whose pelt is frosted with grief. Grief hardens

in its setting apart, eyes secret on the crystal and the neon

and silver, set on a kind of voluptuous shock

of someone, not just the pleasure in endlessly cutting

up leaves and paper to confetti, not just the pleasure

of holding up a queue, of disturbing someone hard

at work, but the kind of intoxication you get in military barracks

by banging the lids of bins. Ah, those lollipopped clouds

of dandelion – the seeds of vertigo are all about us.

'I perhaps am secret': Emael sends their eye up

rickety scaffold, into the unstable of it, the careless

rides of pop-up beach amusement park – pandemic?!

It's *high*, remote to see from thence distinct

each thing. Incredibly shit roller-coaster, the head

carriage a green grinning caterpillar head pulling carriages

of its body bearing mostly kids, look at them go, tomorrow

and yesterday mere oceans, screams the only anchor.

The price of them.

        Emael, still shaking off this morning's tiny

landscape of violent attachments, hands in pockets

of outer-space, coasts over closer to buy a ticket.

Play puts the whole of the holiday crowd where something

parental was supposed to be and then smashes

through the screen. Their stomach is dropping

in anticipation, breath is off with disappointed children

trying scared to be hardest. Their bones swell.

They are totally dug up. Who has ever ascended

unscathed, sanguine, from the Underworld?

Who has managed to retrieve their ball

from the Underworld? Emael sees the egg

and feather they buried on that fateful holiday,

the egg and feather their father recognized as crow,

that they buried secret from parents as external soul

glowing with every kind of fire.

                                    And look at them now,

a fabulous success hatched from the impossible,

from the point where all of myself and everything else

could plop into any container, even into a dull bottle

with a narrow neck and weathered dark brown fade to grey.

Anywhere my eye can squeeze, my soft body and the holiday

crowds follow, screaming. They're strapped in loosely

by a burly Traveller, behind two tiny foulmouthed Gala.

They scream already with laughter,

heart, stomach, skin, and lungs, so much another

outside – and they're off! already glimpses of take-off,

here in the Boat of Heaven, with the voice

                                    lacerate

my ears, lacerate my eyes, lacerate my nose, lacerate

my buttocks, for I can take every injury to no wound,

hold stab wounds that do no bleed and then scatter them

with free indirect face with free indirect hands to a crowd
as dandelion seed...

        At the top of the rickety structure
pause for breath and look out to waters tracked
so severally, secretly cut from north to south
and from surface to the depth with motion. Nothing
has been inside you and no one really knows
what sparkles in your trenches, but way back
in your unwary passage you and water share a little salt.
Then wobble downwards, stretch of steel
in warmer weather and a railroad underground, the crowds
cruising, swerving, swirling through plaza with Emael
their feathered inclusion, free, entrained,
up in the air, out of work, making believe that vertigo is real
community since it holds with the general substance
of survival for all and is also social product of all.

        Now we're upside down again, watching
contradiction make out suspended like pigs
in the sky below us. How does *anything* I do escape taboo,
when all is soft and impossible and falling priceless
and impossible from the ground, oozing from its pores,
blushing more tender still with every blow?
Yes, body is scaling, body is stealing the show,
body is stealing away – to silver, to cornelian, to garnet,
to meet a citizen, to meet somebody, to watch the mouth

of their crater. The Sumerian priests are taking selfies:

scream

if you want to go further.

Each step E's eye takes outward
with their body puffs up new fragrance – scent of lavender,
scent of Khaled's fingers, scent of fear boy trampled under
equid hooves – and entrains swarms of ants, thieving tiny
windfalls tiny decorations for the mosaic Standard
at the heart of their eternal city.

Stole song

39.   And so I rest, and after I rest

        my resting against the wall

        is one lamb, while my dancing away

        will be two fat drops of sweat

        on their face, also dancing. You make

        the best robot you can and leave it

        nothing to lean on in this boat

        where you are wearing your best

        clusters of the

                              because of you

        into my own. Let me boast

        of what you have done,

        in the name of the flute robots

        of Sur, rocking on their feet,

        tiny rivulets of panic sweat

        salt trace your beloving features.

                      In the novel proper you saw through

        to hot feet in the dunes and resin weeps

        from melting pine tree.

        I longed to speak out but my voice

        so strong I could not always

        proper. I do not know what always is

        even when my umbilical wire was

        cut, but when I lift my arms

        I have beautiful fingers and can feel

how you glisten here

a fine silver mask of hardened sweat

lift face just off skin stick skin.

                              Buzz in

coat-check queue starts up

it's got to be a shame

I dance, they lift their arms

before in the novel any person hits

the floor. But here I may fall

and am not afraid to fall

and so won't fall. I feel movements

and am not always the feeling but I do

what it tells me, so am in touch

with fabulous words and love using

my thighs with them. I am as a journal

without money, fearless of Stock

Exchanges, and on earth I move

swiftly, providing us with thin air

and shining of the sun.

Out of the taxi, crashing through

the sheets of plastic visibility, I am in

and out of jobs, I float 'sharp' just out

of reach of outside myself,

of what we know, of the actual instant

music started up out of thin air.

But you, I would sweeten tiny

cheeses for you, give you the lettuce

I have watered of myself. Let me boast

you more: your dancefloor planks

are flood-currents flashing together

in pure Euphrates; your podium a lofty

dais; your engine a simmering interior

mountain of abundance; your beams

are soldiers ready to strike other

soldiers; your prow is brave break

with day, beating its breast against any

heaving waves. Enormous plants

and fruits appear and they have no

similarity to objects; the view through

doorways to sheer mercantile distance

of the outside world is a slap

in the face. Turn back into the vessel

shimmy down on prow

through sharp spray.

                Limited time

implies a kind of rhythm, scaffolding

for dance moves, tender things establishing

routes beyond themselves. Rhythm

a form of building I rhythm

back to tent to city rhythm breathings

and never hail a person before divining

their rhythm through my skin and all

three hearts.

Before the name slaps

on the face as pages badly shut there is a brain

hurting in every dance move,

remembering and tasting, all eye

all screen, making listening of us tasty

to loss and care. It feasts me up to you.

I loss in to you – the while of you,

the look of you, even the not-now

and no wound of you.

Even when you lazy novel

plump for forests, strike tent evocative,

when you hollow underwater city,

it banlieue, it news of glass

crumbling hard from sky,

it bark on sea. Each time it double past:

past leading up to it

past that lives on,

while you route out rhythms between.

I want to have faults because I want to help

people. Now let us sing

as nightbird sing. Night in nightclub

winging plastic smoke and hot sobs

nightbird sing:

   take give keep care hold well clear.

Or lonely morning foot of cliff

on waters broken coast breached

nightbird sing:

   give give care clear take hold well.

Longing persons everywhere and city

blocking every movement *to*,

nightbird mocking sing:

   hold care keep keep clear take hold.

Listening of us made doubt

over limits. If this is nightbird lyric

push thorn in nightbird spleen

to make it sing. If this is novel,

nightbird writing novel:

   hold well keep care give take give

into your own. Let the fabulous words

hover at your ear then take them in your beak

and swallow them to open faults

between yourself. Open show song

of this capacity for broken:

                    to rove

to rise up to fall down are yours

my loves to run to companion

to give are yours to escape

to diminish to know that you have flashing eyes

all yours to vibrate fast

as a person can feel vibrations.

Having no starting point was stolen

song. Once again

                           Leaving me with nothing

makes me fond and personal,

face scarred by lusty fever shell pierces

soft wound deep sea swells into ear,

the grain of voice untradable

in this scale, as if millions had taken part

in song to pour it out in bits of unison

through one small beak sharp notes

with melty voice. In their sweet dividing throat

they winter against water quench,

evade police process (harden

to a brittle shield of song

which dull cracks captured for compatibility,

song sold, soft boy smeared

wounded boy across the screen).

No several lung so stupid: song stole slips

through seeing all the way down

to catacombs and underworld of voice

singing how a face is eye rhyme

of other faces, a real thing, an attachment

to something that hasn't yet occurred

to you. Stick to what you don't know.

Passage flightlines out and mighty

love pours terrifying violent songbot

through these tiny holes – rhythm really is

a dancer of such sweet breach.

When a thief leaves a breach they give

themselves away. Come take

to the dancer. Come take to the breach.

Come clean in this same boat

not boat to liquid notes that close

the eye of Day. Skin flushing song

across the clouds that also pass,

minds squeezing against empty tanks

where flashing silver open mouths kiss air

LAY OUT YOUR UNREST

www.ingramcontent.com/pod-product-compliance
Lightning Source LLC
Chambersburg PA
CBHW021144090426
42740CB00008B/930